"One thing I do know. I was blind but now I see" (John 9:25).

*Others Who Have Been to John of God
Comment on* TO SEE AS GOD SEES

"I found it very interesting. The more I read the more I wanted to find out. Well done! I would call this a masterpiece. Somehow it reminded me of Chico Xavier who wrote over 400 books, and then again, he had eyesight problems—amazing!"
—Chantal Helene, Life Coach, Clinical Hypnotherapist
Brittany, France

"A rich documentation of the inner experiences and visions that accompany the spiritual path, especially one of exploring the who, why, and what of this current life/incarnation...not a typical storyline...incredible shares of the vastness of one soul's journey and visions."

—Debra Sensel, Life Coach, HR Professional,
Healing Practitioner, Lover of God . . .
Reston, Virginia

"So timely, as so many of us seem to be in the metamorphosis process of emergence. Dr. Jackson shares his commitment to be whole. This journey of his visionary experience can only serve to empower and validate his readers as we traverse these most interesting of times."

—William L. Perlman, B.A., J.D., fellow traveler
Dallas, Texas

"One of Dr. Jackson's many gifts is to dwell daily in a place of the recognition and spiritual power of seemingly random events, and to *see* how they guide and reinforce our spiritual path and act as guideposts along the way if we only learn to pay attention to them. The type of seeing that guides him may indeed be more valuable than the eyesight that many of us take for granted."
—Sharon Simmons, Director, Angel in the House
Village of Arden, Delaware

"I really, really enjoyed this book! It confirmed many of the realizations I've had and found so helpful on my spiritual path . . .
—Susanne Newrkla, Journalist
Vienna, Austria

TO SEE
AS
GOD
SEES

Also by Dr. Stephen Royal Jackson

The Space Between Stars
*The Magical Space Where
Stars & Miracles Are Born*

8 Steps to Love
*How to Return to Love When You
Need It the Most—the Moment
Stress & Conflict Begin*

A Matter of Love
*A Fascinating Journey About Following &
Fulfilling Your Divine Destiny*

Words Become Flesh
*True Stories of How Words
Hidden in Your Heart Become
The Flesh of Your Life*

Love Conquers Stress
*Applying the 8 Steps to Love
to Various Kinds of Stress*

Love, Stress & Sex
*Applying the 8 Steps to Love
to the Stress of Love & Sex*

Slay the Dragon—Not Each Other
*A Guide to Help You Vanquish the Inner
Source of Stress, Anxiety, Anger & Conflict*

TO SEE
AS
GOD
SEES

*A Quest for Restored Vision
Becomes an Eye-Opening Adventure*

Stephen Royal Jackson, Ph.D.

Published by
SET Publishing
Wilmington, Delaware

TO SEE AS GOD SEES
Copyright © 2013 First Edition
by Stephen Royal Jackson, Ph.D.

All rights reserved. This book, or part thereof, may
not be reproduced in any form without permission.

For information address:
SET Publishing, Inc.
2304 Riddle Avenue
Suite 406
Wilmington, Delaware 19806

Cataloging-in-Publication Data is available
from the Library of Congress

Cover Design by Jennifer McVeigh of Aztec Printing & Design
Cover image, aptly entitled, *The Eye of God,*
is from a photo taken by the Hubble Telescope.

Printed in the United States of America

Dedicated To

All my dear friends, both seen and unseen,
and to Janet who has truly been and ever shall be
God's Gracious Gift

A Special Thank You
For the invaluable
input of my editor
Betty Bell Harker

Author's Note

I prefer to use *we* instead of *you* in addressing each individual reader of my books because we are all in this together. At times, in order to convey that I am dealing with the same human situation, I may deviate from standard grammatical convention. For example, I may say something like, "when we open our heart and mind, we can really hear each other better." I pair the plural pronoun *our* with singular nouns *heart* and *mind*. At a deeper level, this deviation is in sync with the emerging awareness that we are essentially interconnected and all one spiritually and scientifically at the subatomic level. The Mayan shamans emphasized that we are all one, and not one of us is to be left behind in the great shift of consciousness predicted by the Maya thousands of years ago.

You will see the English name Jesus is replaced by Yeshua, His Middle Eastern name. The exception to this is when someone is being quoted and that individual uses the name Jesus. The deeper reason will be disclosed in chapter six. Also, please note the following deviations from the rules of grammar. Personal and possessive pronouns relating to God in the Christian Trinity are capitalized. Heaven is also capitalized. Something seems awry when Heaven is not capitalized when mentioned in a sentence with planet Earth. Surely, Heaven deserves equal billing with Earth.

CONTENTS

About the Author ii
Dear Reader iii

Prologue: Oprah & Sophia? 1

I
Before Brazil

1. Life on Mars? 7
2. Elizabeths Everywhere? 13
3. Dreaming of a Desert? 18
4. A Mind Divided? 23
5. Unexpected Emissaries? 29

II
Brazil & Beyond

6. Yeshua—Not Jesus? 37
7. No to Nerves? 39
8. A Contrite Knight? 44
9. Ramrod Revision? 50
10. Thunderbolt to the Stars? 56
11. The Void? 61
12. Reveal & Remove? 65
13. The Octagon Room? 70
14. Surrendered Seeing? 78
15. Turning It Over? 83

Epilogue: Feel to Heal? 94

ABOUT THE AUTHOR

Dr. Stephen Royal Jackson has been a stress specialist since 1980 when he completed his dissertation on stress and received his doctorate in clinical and child psychology from the University of Virginia.

Late in 1995, Dr. Jackson had a life-changing spiritual experience which led him to leave the clinical practice of psychology a year later. In 1998, he founded SET (Stress Effectiveness Training) for Life Seminars.

Through his writing and seminars, Dr. Jackson is dedicated to helping people all over the world eliminate the needless suffering and senseless evil caused by ineffective ways of handling stress and conflict.

To this end, Dr. Jackson lectures and conducts seminars, and he has often appeared on national television and radio. Since 1995, he has been using a Christian—inspired and guided by the Holy Spirit—form of the deeply relaxing ancient healing art of Reiki. With the healing power of the Holy Spirit working through him, he has helped many people here and abroad find relief from stress and stress-related pain and disease.

DEAR READER

TO SEE AS GOD SEES IS TO SEE WITH TOTAL LOVE and no fear. "When you can see through the eyes of God with total love and no fear, then your vision will become clear," whispered the still small voice within. This revelation occurred during my time with the Mayan shamans over a decade ago and has been the lofty goal directing my quest to have my severely damaged vision restored. I have been astonished at all that has crossed my path to guide me. The synchronicity has been amazing. Books, television shows, films, visions and dreams, a phrase on a billboard, a street sign, the casual comment of a stranger have all been part of my quest. Everything has been expanding my concept of what restoring my vision truly means, what is illusion, and what is reality. Through all this, I have come to see the way to truly feeling good and being at peace involves the ultimate stress relief of remembering who we *really* are. All of this will be revealed to you as you accompany me on my quest. I am especially grateful for being guided to the following for having furthered my advances on the path to restoring my vision: Gary Renard's audio book *The Disappearance of the Universe*; Eckhart Tolle's *A New Earth*, the television detective series *Life on Mars*; Jungian analyst Dr. Karlyn Ward for her DVD presentation *Anchored in the Heart*; Mary Baker Eddy's classic *Science & Health*; Anita Moorjani's *Dying to be Me*; Dr. Wayne Dyer's report of his distant healing experience with John of God; and the divinely-delivered *A Course in Miracles*.

—*Stephen Royal Jackson, Ph.D.*
New Year's Day
January 1, 2011

What I have chosen to see has cost me vision. Now I will choose again that I may see.
—Workbook Lesson 52 in *A Course in Miracles*

It breaks the dream of disease to understand that sickness is formed by the human mind, not by matter nor by the Divine Mind.
—Mary Baker Eddy, *Science & Health*

Realize that your forgiveness entitles you to vision. Understand that the Holy Spirit never fails to give the gift of sight to the forgiving. . . . He will show you what true vision sees…Rejoice in the power of forgiveness to heal your sight completely.
—Workbook Lesson 75 in *A Course in Miracles*

Prologue

Oprah & Sophia?

JANUARY 1, 2011

SOMETHING THAT COULD BE BEST DESCRIBED AS AN energy shift is beginning to arise from the depths of the heart of humanity. Examples of this shift abound everywhere. Witness the following. Dan Brown's *Da Vinci Code* weaves a mystery based on that earthy redhead Mary Magdalene having created a bloodline with Jesus. The film *The Black Swan* portrays a ballerina's struggle to embrace the repressed qualities expressed in the image of the black swan. Spiritual teacher Eckhart Tolle teaches us of the importance of shifting our focus from DOING to BEING. The best-selling book *The Shack* depicts God as an earth-mother in the form of a large, wise and deeply loving black woman. The empress of the talk show genre, Oprah Winfrey, has just this very day launched her OWN television network. What is the deeper energy shift of which the above are but mere waves and ripples?

Over five decades ago, the famous Swiss psychiatrist, C. G. Jung, predicted that there would be a reemergence of the ancient images of the archetypal feminine in the new millennium. Jung saw this as an expression of what he called "the self-regulating nature of the psyche" which applies to both the individual and collective psyche. In my master's thesis *Mandala Symbolism in 19th Century American Romantic Literature*, I described how archetypal images arise in the art and literature of an age. As in the dreams of individuals, these images emerge from the collective unconscious in an effort to make up for what is lacking in the collective consciousness or world view of that age.

This shift to the feminine is taking place after 2000 years of Western Culture being dominated by patriarchal, masculine values. These values are epitomized by an emphasis on DOING and HAVING rather than on simply BEING. The advances in technology reflect what the heroic effort to *do* and to *acquire* can do to improve the quality of life. So much has been done to develop new and better things. However, with the archetypal feminine, come the values of the heart, emotional intelligence and intuition, and the wisdom of the body. These values arise to bring balance after centuries of a one-sided emphasis on the head, the intellect, and reason.

The goddess Sophia leads the pantheon of divine feminine figures. You might say that my love affair with Sophia began in college when I felt a tingling up my spine the very moment the professor told us that *philosophy* meant love of Sophia (the Greek word for wisdom). Thus began a pursuit of wisdom that has remained a lifelong endeavor. I also felt that same tingling when I learned of the centrality of Sophia from a recorded presentation on the long-repressed dark, positive feminine by Jungian analyst, Dr. Karlyn Ward. The presentation was aptly named *Anchored in the Heart*. The dark feminine refers both to divine feminine figures who have been kept in the dark over the centuries and to the feminine values and qualities they embody and symbolize.

Sophia has remained hidden in plain sight. For example, almost no reference is made to the diminutive female figure in Michelangelo's Creation series on the ceiling of the Sistine Chapel. The figure is Sophia, and she is held to God's side as a bride by one of God's massive arms. With His other arm, God reaches out to touch Adam's finger.

Sophia is associated with the color black, and with the ancient images of the Black Madonna. Wisdom was associated with black because wisdom is often hidden in the dark depths within each one of us.

One afternoon, I was reflecting on Sophia and then a question arose. Who is the most powerful feminine presence of our time?

Oprah. Clearly, she embodies all that is associated with the archetypal dark feminine. She is a dark-skinned woman who has been dispensing daily doses of wisdom for decades. The steady stream of experts she has hosted on her show have provided information to help us heal our lives and relationships. Now, with her OWN television network, Oprah has achieved a kind of omnipresence—an appropriate quality for a modern-day representative of Sophia.

In conducting interviews, Oprah embodies the compassionate, empathic presence of an archetypal earth-mother. Oprah appeared at a time in human history when our lives and relationships were, and still are, in desperate need of the feminine values of compassion, wisdom, and emotional intelligence.

What is being described applies equally to males and females. Just because a woman is in a female body does not mean she is in touch with her heart and the other positive qualities found in the archetypal feminine. She may be driven by the values of our male-dominated society thereby denying all that her deeper feminine nature offers. She may, in effect, behave as if she were a very driven, type A task-oriented man.

In his book *The Essential Mystics*, Andrew Harvey directs our attention to what we all, men or women, need for the next conscious step in human evolution.

> For the human race to have a chance to survive…there has to be a fusion between our masculine and feminine energies…between our innermost mystical awareness and our political, technological and economic choices. Only such a fusion and sacred marriage can produce in us the necessary clarity, knowledge and force of active love necessary to preserve the world.

What follows is the story of how my quest for healing my eyes led me, a typical action-oriented American male, a product of Western Civilization, into unfamiliar territory. What I encountered was totally unexpected but, in retrospect, made perfect sense. It is the story of my descent into the dark depths of my heart where I found the eternal feminine hidden behind a wall of fiercely masculine attitudes.

Prologue

The journey in this book begins where the journey initiated in *The Space Between Stars* leaves off. From there, you will accompany me on both my inward and outward travels. You will go with me and see what I saw on my visits to the healer-medium Joao de Deus (John of God) at the Casa de Dom Inacio de Loyola (the house of St. Ignatius of Loyola) the healing center located in the village of Abadiania, Brazil. Shortly after my arrival at the Casa (the abbreviated way that most staff and visitors affectionately refer to the healing center), I was confronted by visions dating back to the Crusades. All the eye-opening experiences I had on my quest for restored vision will be revealed to you and, hopefully, help you attain true vision which is something other than simply seeing 20/20. . . .

Once again, as I mentioned in the preface, it is to see as the still small voice whispered to me when I was with the Maya: *"When you can see with total love and no fear, your vision will become clear."* For more than a decade, it has been my quest to see as God sees with total love and no fear. This seemingly lofty goal has been the guiding torch I bear, lighting my way through the thorny thickets of the dark-forest night of my damaged vision to the dawn of a new day of seeing EVERYTHING clearly.

* * *

I NOW OFFER A WORD OF CAUTION TO THE LOGICAL left brain of each person reading this book. You, dear left brain, have an affinity for linear logic. And this affinity is of great assistance in the conduct of our daily lives. Therefore, it is important to note that, while offering a chronology of my eye-opening experiences, the dates at the beginning of each chapter are mere launching pads for the rockets of insights that will hopefully take you to new heights of awareness. You will find that I segue into themes that emerged on different trips to Brazil so the events discussed in each chapter are not confined to that one day in my life. I hope you enjoy the ride you are about to take and find it in some way enlightening.

I
Before Brazil

The time-bound mode of consciousness is deeply embedded in the human psyche. But what we are doing here is part of a profound transformation taking place in the collective consciousness of the planet and beyond, the awakening of consciousness from the *dream of matter, form, and separation,* the ending of time. [Italics added] We are breaking mind patterns that have dominated human life for aeons, mind patterns that have created unimaginable suffering on a vast scale.
—Eckhart Tolle, *The Power of Now*

The physical universe expresses the conscious and unconscious thoughts of mortals.
—Mary Baker Eddy, *Science & Health*

When morning comes, this one knows that the fear that had been experienced was nothing. . . . Since there had been fear and confusion…and double mindedness and division, there were many illusions that were conceived by them [the unawakened]…as if they were fast asleep and found themselves prey to troubled dreams. Either they are fleeing somewhere, or they lack strength to escape when pursued. They are involved in inflicting blows…Other times, it is as if certain people were trying to kill them, even though there is no one pursuing them; or they themselves are killing those beside them…Until the moment when they who are passing through all these things…awaken, they see nothing because the dreams were nothing…And happy is the one who comes to himself and awakens. Indeed, blessings on the one who has opened the eyes of the blind
—Valentinos, "WAKING UP AND COMING TO KNOWLEDGE," *The Gospel of Truth,* circa 2nd century C.E.

One

Life on Mars?

MARCH 25, 2009

"I can't believe that none of that about his father and mother and himself as a little boy was real!" Nick exclaimed. My good buddy Nick was disturbed by the final episode of the TV series *Life on Mars*. Nick's reaction reminded me of the words of Yeshua's advice to His disciples in the Gospel of Thomas which I had recently read. (Note: Yeshua, the more historically accurate Hebrew name of Jesus, will be used throughout this book instead of Jesus, and, in chapter six, I'll explain its special meaning.)

> Let the one who seeks not stop seeking until he finds. When he finds, he will become troubled. And when he becomes troubled, he will be astonished and rule over all things.

Like the seeker described above in saying number 2 of the Gnostic Gospel of Thomas, Nick was "troubled" by the discovery that the true identity of Sam, the main character in the series, was not that of a detective in New York City. At the same time, we were both astonished by Sam's true identity which I'll disclose later. This TV series was laying out the steps I needed to take on my healing journey to restore my sight.

The series centered on Sam (Jason O'Mara), a New York City police detective in 2008 who, after being knocked unconscious, wakes up as a New York City detective in 1973. Curiously, this was the year I began Jungian analysis, and I remember my analyst responding to some synchronicity I shared with him by saying,

"We get our messages from the damnedest places." Surely, the finale of a TV detective series is an unlikely place from which to receive spiritual direction. And now, in retrospect, 1973 qualifies as the formal inception of my spiritual quest. The classic film *The Wizard of Oz* is a beautiful depiction of the quest. Ripped out of her home in Kansas, Dorothy lands in Oz and all her efforts and adventures involve trying to find a way to get back to her home. Allusions to Dorothy and Oz are woven into the fabric of each episode of *Life on Mars*. Similar to Dorothy's desire to return home to Kansas, Sam's sole goal is to find a way to return home to his life in 2008. But in the confluence of concepts crossing my path, I would see that the metaphysical level of the journey involves how we, as spiritual beings, leave our home in Heaven to be born in a body on Earth. Finding our way back to our home in Heaven is our primary goal whether we realize it consciously or not. And, as I would soon come to see, Heaven is within us; it is a state of consciousness we can all achieve on Earth.

Sam's story also involves the psychological theme of Sam's coming to terms with his earthly father. This element of the show paralleled the psychological aspects of what I needed to *see* and resolve in my childhood, relating to my father. In exploring the emotional roots of my glaucoma, I had to come to terms with my early childhood and my relationship with my father. I presented this part of my healing journey in *Words Become Flesh* and *The Space Between Stars*. My purpose here is to pick up where these books left off and focus on the spiritual phase of my healing journey.

In this final episode, I would witness Sam reconciling with what could be called his father in the starry heavens. I'll explain this later in this chapter. Resolving the estranged relationship between father and son mirrors the biblical parable of *The Prodigal Son*. Soon I would learn that this parable was the next step in my spiritual search for restored sight. I would also see that it expresses the essence of the spiritual quest of every soul.

In his work as a detective in 1973, Sam encounters his mother Rose and father Vic, and, as an adult male in his thirties, Sam has a talk with himself as little five-year-old Sammy. He revisits his memories of his father's abandoning both him and his mother.

In the opening scene of the series finale, Sam picks up the phone at his desk which is situated in the middle of the police squad room at the 125th precinct. The anonymous voice on the other end tells Sam that he must do three things if he wants to return home. The first is to save himself. Sam is puzzled but seconds later his mother Rose appears by Sam's desk. She is frantic. Sam's father Vic has abducted little five-year-old Sammy, and Sam's mother Rose asks Sam for help. Somehow, the call for Sam to save himself as a child seemed significant spiritually. This call is symbolic of the spiritual call to awaken. I would soon hear it said that we all receive this call from the part of our mind inhabited by the voice for God, the Holy Spirit, calling us home. More specifically, we all need to save the loving, innocent child in us. As Yeshua once said, "Truly, I say to you, unless you become like children, you will never enter the kingdom of heaven" (Matthew 18:3-5). Here we have the archetypal feminine (Rose) asking Sam to rescue the innocent child (Sammy) from the aggressive masculine gone out of control (Vic).

I smile to myself as I reflect on the names of Sam's parents. *The name Rose reminds me of the beautiful and fragrant flower that is a perennial symbol of love. In contrast, Vic reminds me of the word* vic *in cop shows which is short for* victim. *And, isn't it the victim in us all who feels angry, bitter, and resentful?* Soon, I would learn how we all need to replace the role of victim with the willingness to assume full responsibility for our lives.

A few hours after writing the above, I was riding in the car of my friend Rod, an Episcopal priest. (Rod was instrumental in my going to Brazil to see John of God). The instant I asked Rod about the rose as a symbol of spiritual love, he pointed to the large sign in front of a church we were passing by. It featured a rose on a cross with the words, "Celebrate God's Love." God was winking.

Following Rose's hunch about where Vic might have taken Sammy, Sam finds himself in the quaint little seaside town of Hyde where he was conceived. Sam steps into a phone booth and calls the precinct to request back-up from his fellow officers. The call is interrupted. An electronically disguised voice cuts in and says, "Back to the egg, where it all begins and ends."

Sam's return to the place where he was conceived would prove significant when I thought back to what I had just read the day before in the *Gospel of Thomas*. Yeshua was quoted as saying, "Blessed is he who knows the beginning." And, "Blessed is the one who came into being before he came into being."

I was stunned. These words of Yeshua and Sam's symbolic return to before his birth tied in directly with the beginning of *The Space Between Stars* in which I recount the reliving of my own prebirth experience during a healing session. It also correlated with what I would later discover to be a core teaching of a book given to me just days after this series finale. The book was *The Disappearance of the Universe*. I'll say more about this in later chapters.

The voice whispers the second instruction that Sam needs to follow if he is to return home. "You gotta duck. Just duck!" Sam ducks in the nick of time as shots are fired and bullets shatter the glass at the top of the phone booth.

Sam races from the scene to track Vic and Sammy to a ship docked at the local harbor. Vic suddenly appears and Sam tells Vic, "I'm gonna take you in, Vic." I could see in this confrontation the need to restrain the aggressive male in all of us, whether we are a male or a female. The spiritual journey home involves coming to terms with our anger and learning to forgive and find peace.

Vic replies, "That's not gonna happen. We're gonna get out of Dodge, Sammy and I, father and son, and we're gonna come back and eat all the butter and eggs in New York City." There's that egg theme again. The egg is a symbol of the origin of life.

Speaking for little Sammy, Sam tells Vic how Sammy worships Vic and how Sammy is afraid of "the darkness" in Vic. However, Sam proclaims how he isn't afraid.

Sam and Vic begin to fight. They tumble onto the deck of the ship. First, Sam knocks Vic down and is on top of Vic. Then Vic maneuvers to be on top of Sam. Before Vic makes his move to kill him, Sam tells Vic he can't kill him, and Vic asks why. Sam replies, "Because I'm your son."

Vic acknowledges that he knows Sam is his son. Pinning Sam to the deck of the ship with his knees on Sam's arms, Vic rears back with a long knife to stab and kill Sam but Gene (Harvey Keitel), Sam's supervisor at the 125th precinct arrives in time to shoot and kill Vic. Later, I would see this rescue as revealing another key part of what I needed to see in my own healing and the universal spiritual truth to which it points. This will be clear when the true identities of both Gene and Sam are revealed.

Back at the police station, Sam answers the phone on his desk. The same unknown man's voice he has heard before tells him, "One more thing, just one more thing and you're home, Sam." Sam interrupts the man and indicates he's not interested in going home. This acceptance of his circumstances would also prove to be a key part of the spiritual path.

Sam professes how much he likes 1973 and then he says, "You know what, pal, maybe I don't want to go home so badly anymore. How do ya like that? Huh? 'Cause I like 1973 and everybody in it and because a long time ago, someone I love once told me, 'Whichever strange place you find yourself in, make that your home.'" Sam slams down the phone.

Across the room, Gene calls Sam over, saying, "I need to talk to you, Tyler [Sam's last name]." Sam crosses the room, enters Gene's office, and, before Gene can say anything to Sam, Sam promptly hugs Gene. Alluding to *The Wizard of Oz*, Gene says, "I think I'm gonna miss you most of all, Scarecrow." The transmission of the picture on the television screen starts to break up and fades to black; it's as though there is some kind of electronic interference.

The scene shifts from the New York City police squad room set in 1973 to a spaceship preparing to land on Mars in 2035.

Sam and other members of his squad comprise the crew aboard a spaceship. Each one emerges from his own capsule, containing a life-support system. They have all been sleeping and dreaming for over two years. Similar to Dorothy in the final scene of *The Wizard of Oz*, Sam recounts his time-traveling dream to the rest of the crew, describing how they were all there with him in 1973.

The ship commander, Major Tom, formerly Gene, Sam's supervisor in 1973, climbs out of his capsule. The crew is about to step onto Martian soil. But, before they do, Sam approaches Major

Tom. The ship's commander turns out to be his actual father from whom he has been estranged. Sam stands before his father and suggests they set aside their differences, saying, "So, uh, before we do this amazing thing, I just wanna say that, uh, I really don't wanna fight with you anymore, Dad." Major Tom steps a little closer, and, affectionately cradles Sam's face, and says, "Life is good, Kiddo. It's like I've been telling you since you were a little boy, whichever strange place you land in, make that your home." Major Tom's words echo the advice of all spiritual teachers: accept what is, or, as Harvard's guru Ram Dass said it, "Be here now."

So Sam's real identity is that of an astronaut, not a cop. His real need is to reconcile with Major Tom, who is his father in the starry heavens in contrast to Vic, his earthly father in his dream. A very important spiritual truth is revealed here. It is Sam's father in the heavens who saves him from Vic and who subdues the aggressive male. The conflict between earthly father and son must be transcended and resolved spiritually rather than by the son subduing the father with force.

Months later I would be led to paraphrase God's words to St. Paul (2 Corinthians 12:7). I addressed God by praying, "Thank You that Your power is made perfect in my weakness." I saw how there was a spiritual step that involved not fighting our anger. Instead, we need to surrender our swords and seek the power of God's peace. Whether male or female, we all carry anger as part of the human experience, and we can release that anger spiritually into God's hands. As I will explain further in chapter seven, it was on my first trip to Brazil that I saw how my anger took the form of impatience and was related to my having a Type A Personality.

God winked as I was writing the above with the television on in the background. I smiled as I heard minister Joyce Meyer admit having a problem with being impatient. She then announced, "Impatience is the greatest weakness of the Type A Personality." Bingo. For me, the letter A in Type A relates to my addiction to accomplishment, to *doing*, instead of *being*. When obstacles appear, the desire to accomplish leads to anger and its derivatives—impatience and grievances. In Brazil, I would see that releasing ancient grievances was to be part of my healing journey.

Two
Elizabeths Everywhere?

APRIL 24, 2009

The day before the 2008 presidential election, I sent a copy of the first draft of my book, *The Space Between Stars* to my college basketball coach Dan Peterson who was living in Milan, Italy. Right after I left the post office, I stopped by the local coffee shop and unexpectedly saw my friend Andy. I told him I had just mailed a copy of my latest book to my college coach since part of the book was devoted to basketball. Andy and I began reminiscing about our high school basketball days. He mentioned how cohesive his high school team had been. Listening to his description of his team, I was reminded of a very cohesive post-season tournament team on which I played.

I was a freshman in college and both the college and high school seasons had ended. It was the second semester of my freshman year at the University of Virginia, and I had contracted pneumonia and had to drop out of school for the rest of the semester. By the time of the tournament, I had recovered enough to play a little post-season basketball. I told Andy how the team was composed of players from a legendary undefeated St. Elizabeth's High School team. I was plugged into this cohesive team, and we won the tournament against an impressive array of players from Rutgers University, West Virginia University, and Providence College.

After speaking to Andy, I thought of Richie, the superb playmaker who was a major factor in fostering the team's cohesiveness

I had so admired. The next day, I was stunned when I received an e-mail. The subject line read: "Greetings from Barcelona." It was from Richie (now Rich), that talented ball-handler and outstanding playmaker from that well-oiled machine of a team from forty years earlier. Rich had just had lunch with my coach who had told Rich about my new book. Rich was eager to read it since it made reference to my basketball experiences. How amazing it was that a day earlier I had spoken about that post-season tournament we had played in, and now I was hearing from him after forty years.

In my daily inner conversation with God, what I had come to call my daily dialogue with the Divine, I wondered if there was anything significant about Rich being from St. Elizabeth's instead of one of the other area schools. I asked myself, *Who was St. Elizabeth?*

Suddenly, I thought of the Visitation, the second joyful mystery on the Rosary. Mary was pregnant with Yeshua when she paid a visit to her cousin Elizabeth who was pregnant with John the Baptist. I recalled how I always loved the way the visit is described in the Bible: Elizabeth was carrying John in her womb when he "leapt for joy" at sensing the presence of Yeshua in Mary's womb. Reflecting on how that scene related to hearing from Rich, I saw the connection. Rich's enthusiasm for my book reminded me of the prebirth joy John felt. Here I was about to give birth to my latest book which included how Christ had impacted my life and spiritual path. What Mother Maria del Carmen had said about *8 Steps to Love*, my first book, also applied to the book about to be released: "Reading this book helps us fulfill the commandment of love that Jesus gave us."

As I thought about it further, I recalled that I had recently written a prayer in honor of Mary. Viewing the Catholic television network, EWTN, I was taken by the notion of Mary as the model disciple. She had said yes to God which resulted in giving birth to Yeshua. Mary seemed to be the best symbol for how we all manifest spirit in matter, that is, to manifest from the spiritual into the material. The Word of Love became flesh in Mary. I was moved one morning by Louis de Mumford's prayer claiming Mary as his mother and queen. This is the prayer I wrote that claimed Mary as a model for me:

> Holy Mary Mother of God, thank you for saying yes to God and giving birth to Yeshua (Jesus). For by saying yes to God, you helped bring forth the incarnation, our redemption, and salvation, and you provided for us a model for manifesting the spirit love in matter. Holy Mary, Mother of God, pray for me as I pray: 'Father God, please help me be as on fire with faith and as fearless as Mary so that I, too, may say yes to You; and through the power of Your Holy Spirit give birth to Yeshua in the manger of my heart every moment of this day, and have the love of Christ reign in everything I think, feel, say, and do.

I was now seeing Mary as a model for manifesting the spiritual in the material. It is the feminine within us that manifests or gives birth to what we would love to have happen in our lives. We are all both Mary and Elizabeth. As Mary, we bring the spirit of Christ, our true self, into the world of form; and as Elizabeth, we carry the John in us that celebrates, that is, leaps for joy, when we witness and encourage each other to bring forth the spirit of love, the Christ, within us into the world.

After all these years, Rich was doing that by showing an excited interest in my book which, as with all my books, brings the message of love, the commandment that Yeshua gave us. Love is who we are and love is what we need to return to when anger, fear, sadness and depression threaten to overwhelm us. My new book was revealing how I had come to this position.

Then it hit me; I realized there had been another Liz (Elizabeth) helping on my healing journey. Three years earlier the first Elizabeth had appeared. She is the sister of Greer, one of my oldest and dearest friends. Greer and I go back to sixth grade. The film *Stand by Me* reminds me of him since we were the same age as the boys depicted in the movie; the last line in the movie says something about the main character, now an adult (Richard Dreyfus), "I never had friends like the ones I had at twelve . . . does anybody?" Liz and Greer had just lost their father, and I had just had my second of what would be three surgeries on my eyes. Greer asked Liz to help me out with appointments and such since I was no longer able to drive. Greer knew that assigning Liz to assist me would get her mind off her loss and it did. Liz was also part of an Episcopal prayer group and Bible study. Following my eye surgeries, I spent four years attending the Bible study meetings with Liz. In that time, I had deepened my knowledge and understanding of the Bible.

A few weeks after hearing from Rich, I was having a conversation with Suzanne, one of my editors. I was telling her about my idea of how we all need to be both a *manifesting* Mary and an *encouraging* Elizabeth. She smiled, laughed, and informed me, "Elizabeth is my middle name." She certainly qualified as an encouraging Elizabeth in my life. Her editing had encouraged me to refine some of my thinking and her invaluable input had helped me grow spiritually.

Flash ahead five months. As has always happened thus far on my spiritual journey in general and vision quest or healing journey, I experience something unusual and then I find confirmation of my experience. One late afternoon in April, I was walking out of *Eeffoc*, the local coffee shop whose quirky name is coffee spelled backwards. I nearly bumped into a young woman named Liz (Elizabeth). Five months earlier, she and I had met after she had prayed to meet a Reiki healer with a Christ-oriented approach to the ancient healing art. Given her lifelong feelings of closeness to Christ, she had prayed for someone with a similar affinity for Him. On this spring afternoon, Liz was excited to tell me about a book that included many quotes from Christ and could be considered a modern version of *The Gospel of Thomas*. It had a provocative title: *The Disappearance of the Universe.*

Fortunately, she had an audio copy of the book so I could listen to it. I had lost my ability to see well enough to read four years earlier. An audio book was perfect. I qualified for the services of the Division of the Visually Impaired, and I regularly received audio books in the mail. The book Liz gave me highlighted the teachings from the self-study program in spiritual psychotherapy entitled *A Course in Miracles*. This audio book had many quotations attributed to Yeshua that were taken from the Course and some that came from the Gospel of Thomas. A year later, I would download a copy of the Course from the National Library for the Blind. I listened to the entire text of this self study course which was over six hundred pages. I completed my first listening and study of the text one month before going on my second trip to Brazil to see John of God. A few months after my return from Brazil, I would embark on the 365 daily lessons in the workbook section of the Course.

Now the divine feminine was operating through another Liz. This other Elizabeth was guiding me on my healing journey by giving me a book that would help me make sense of the prebirth experience I had relived during a shamanic workshop over a decade ago. It was interesting to me how this audio book would take me full circle. It would take me back to where my spiritual path became a more conscious quest. It was when I became interested in the writings of Carl Jung and began delving into dreams. Only now the emphasis was on waking up from the dream instead of analyzing it.

Meanwhile, I didn't know it then but three years later, I'd meet yet another Elisabeth who had an *s* in the middle of her name, and, guess what . . . She was from Brazil and she was from a long line of homeopathic doctors. This Elisabeth would guide me more deeply into the healing gifts of the feminine. But for now back to the theme of the dream.

Three

Dreaming of a Desert?

MAY 5, 2009

"You are at home in God, dreaming of exile, but perfectly capable of awakening to reality." Wow! There was the dream theme again. This was the first of three quotations from *The Disappearance of the Universe*. These words were attributed to Yeshua They really rocked my concept of reality. *Life on Mars* had ended with the whole drama being a dream and now Liz had placed a book in my hands that continued the theme. What we consider life is but a dream, and often it's better described as a nightmare. The next quotation attributed to Yeshua clarifies a mysterious passage in *The Gospel of Thomas*. It is said to contain the words Yeshua spoke to St. Thomas when the two went off by themselves. As soon as Thomas returned, the other disciples were eager to hear what the Master had told him. Thomas refused to share what he had been told. He was reluctant to tell them for fear they would "stone" him. The words would have been considered blasphemy.

> You dream of a desert where mirages are your rulers and tormentors. Yet these images come from you. Father did not make the desert and your home is still with Him. To return, you must forgive your brother for only then do you forgive yourself.

What!? God did not create the universe!? We did!? I'll say more about that later. The Creation Story in the Bible is *not* the true story!? Instead, we are told that the story of *The Prodigal Son* is more in line with what happened. And isn't that interesting because that was the story depicted in the crime drama *Life on Mars.*

I was astonished by the parallels between *The Disappearance of the Universe* and *Life on Mars,* the show with its theme of trying to find a way to get back home along with the exchanges between father and son, and the words attributed to Yeshua in *The Disappearance of the Universe.* Rather than the story of Creation and the Fall, Yeshua suggests that the story of *The Prodigal Son* is a more accurate depiction of what every embodied soul goes through in separating or appearing to separate from God.

The comments attributed to Yeshua suggested that we are dreaming we are living on Earth but are really at home with our heavenly Father. Sam was dreaming he was living a life on Earth in 1973 but was really comfortably asleep aboard a spacecraft safely soaring in the starry heavens. Similar to the story of *The Prodigal Son,* the storyline of the show ends with Sam being reconciled to his father in a celestial setting: a spaceship landing on a distant planet. Forgiving others and ourselves in the dream which we call life is how we return home to our heavenly Father.

The daily dialogue with the Divine was turning my world topsy turvy and inside out. I could hear that line from the poet T.S. Eliot playing like a song in my head. He had said something about our ceaseless explorations leading us back to the place where we started and seeing it for the first time. So many things were coming together.

My spiritual journey had begun in 1973 when I entered Jungian analysis with my dream journal in hand. I was fascinated by Jung's interpretation of dreams as containing hidden wisdom from the higher Self within. Dreams were deeply symbolic messages delivered to the ego, the little conscious mind self. Now, nearly four decades later, I see a TV series supposedly set in 1973 in which a man named Sam is trying to get back home. Only his whole life in the series is a dream from which he awakens to find himself on a spaceship landing on Mars.

Next, I am given a book (*The Disappearance of the Universe*) that tells me that Yeshua delivered an inner dictation to Helen Schuchman, a medical psychologist at Columbia University's College of

Physicians and Surgeons. This inner dictation is said to have taken place from 1971 until 1977. Deeply symbolic dreams preceded the inner dictation of what became *A Course in Miracles*. I was coming full circle back to my fascination with dreams in the 1970s. Only now life and the whole universe itself was the dream.

The Disappearance of the Universe and *A Course in Miracles* were saying this world we look upon is essentially a dream, and we are comfortably asleep in God's arms but we don't know it. Similarly, each night when we sleep and dream, we don't know we are safely tucked in our bed. The nightmare of being chased is very real and our physiology responds with an increased heart rate. The only escape is to wake up. Or, is it?

Of course, we can become aware that we are dreaming while we are in a dream. It's a phenomenon called *lucid dreaming*. Either way, we wake up. We wake up completely to find we are safe in our bed or we wake up enough in the dream to realize we are dreaming. We can then take control of events in the dream. For example, I was once dreaming that I was underwater, and I was floating a few feet above the bottom of the lake. I was breathing easily. But then, for a moment, I was startled that I could breathe. Immediately, I thought to myself, *Oh, I'm dreaming*. Suddenly, I saw an ominous shadowy figure coming toward me.

I remembered what Carlos Castaneda had written about dealing with fear in dreams. His spiritual teacher, a Yaqui Indian shaman, told Castaneda, "Look at your hands." Right at that moment in the dream, I looked at my hands. My palms looked especially white as streaks of sunlight penetrated the sepia-tinged water. The shadowy threat instantly vanished.

On another occasion, I was falling from a skyscraper set in some unknown city. It was dark as I plummeted to what would be certain death when I hit the pavement below. While I was falling, I began tensing my muscles as I braced myself for impact. Then I realized I was dreaming. Instantly. muscles relaxed and I began floating. In a flash, I saw a meadow below me and I began slowly drifting toward the mounds of matted grass as if I were a feather carried by a soft summer breeze. I landed ever so gently. A little later, I would hear from *The Disappearance of the Universe* and *A Course in Miracles* something that corresponded with lucid dreaming. There is a step before completely waking up. This step involves changing the nightmare into a happy dream.

As you may recall, my friend Nick was disappointed when the final episode of *Life on Mars* disclosed that Sam's dramatic struggle in confronting his childhood was not real. I reminded Nick that dreams are very real when we are dreaming them, especially nightmares. When we wake up, we find the dream fades but it was no less real. In line with dreams being both real and unreal, I shared with Nick what I learned from Tacomi, a Tibetan Buddhist monk. The following is from *Words Become Flesh*:

'Emptiness and compassion are the two pillars that show us the way out of our suffering,' Tacomi said.

'But how can we feel compassion for people or any being, a dog for that matter, since all beings are empty? Insubstantial? Unreal?'

Tacomi prefaced what he was about to tell me, 'What I am about to say may seem contradictory. As we touched on last time, the Buddha taught us that our self, our I and other beings are not ultimately real. Self and other are impermanent, insubstantial, in essence, empty. In the *Vimalakirti Nirdesa Sutra*, Vimalakirti, a simple man with a wife and children begins by telling Manjushri, an enlightened being, how a bodhisattva views all beings as empty.'

'Let me see if I understand the concept of a bodhisattva,' I interrupted. 'My understanding is that a bodhisattva is an enlightened being who is liberated from the round of birth and death. He does not have to incarnate anymore. Yet he does return because of a great love and compassion for the suffering of others. The bodhisattva comes back to earth to help other beings get free.'

'Yes, that's a good understanding,' Tacomi said. 'As I was saying, Vimalakirti tells Manjushri, *A bodhisattva should regard all beings as a wise man regards the following: the image of a face in the mirror, a bubble in a stream, the image of the moon reflected in a pond, a ball of foam on water, the fleeting sound of an echo, a mirage of water on a desert, and clouds passing in the sky.* Manjushri then asks, *Noble sir, if a bodhisattva considers all living beings in such a way, how does he generate the great love toward them?'*

'Good question,' I said. 'Seeing beings as insubstantial, as empty as balls of foam or passing clouds, how does a bodhisattva generate the great love that is a refuge for all beings? How do we feel love for our loved ones as balls of foam?'

'Essentially,' Tacomi said, 'Vimalakirti explains to Manjushri that a bodhisattva thinks of how living beings *feel real* to themselves. They *feel* the pain of their problems. And the bodhisattva remembers how **real** his own suffering was before he became enlightened. This motivates the bodhisattva to help all beings.'

A few days prior to receiving *The Disappearance of the Universe* and watching the final episode of *Life on Mars*, I had an experience that foreshadowed literally and figuratively the third significant quotation from *The Disappearance of the Universe*:: "Deny you are a shadow briefly laid upon a dying world." Strolling along one day, I noticed something that I have seen innumerable times. I noticed my shadow on the walkway in front of me. Only this time, the still small voice within whispered, "When my shadow's in the lead that means my back is to the light. " I turned around and faced the late-afternoon sun. I lost myself in its radiance. My first thoughts were that my shadow is an absence of light formed by the substance and shape of my body. In *The Space Between Stars*, I had written extensively about the difference between having a body-based sense of self versus a spirit-based identity. When I think of myself as a body, I am, in effect, a small absence of light cast upon the ground. When I think of myself as a spirit with a body, I can imagine being able to go beyond the limits of the body. Paranormal phenomena such as telepathy, clairvoyance, and distant healing are not so inconceivable. As time went on, I would eventually see that this shift in emphasis would prove to be an essential ingredient in my healing.

Four

A Mind Divided?

MAY 21, 2009

I WAS STOPPED IN MY TRACKS BY THE CLAIM THAT GOD did not create this world. This seemingly solid world is a dream, an illusion, where, as Yeshua is said to have described to St. Thomas, "mirages are your rulers and tormentors."

The following brief summary, taken from *The Disappearance of the Universe*, describes events that are essentially of such a depth and breadth that they are incomprehensible to our limited intellects. As such, the events are best conveyed as cosmological parables revealing deep mythological and psychological truths. It was said that in the beginning, "God created Christ and they lived in perfect oneness. Christ was said to be an extension of God and the only difference is that God created Christ." The world was said to be created when we, comprising a "tiny aspect of the Christ Mind," imagined what it might be like to separate from God. The Big Bang followed from this imagining and the physical universe came into being. What was then said about the creation correlated with my experience in doing therapy with children who were suffering from separation anxiety.

A small child going off to school for the first time may experience separation anxiety with its mix of guilt, fear, and projected anger. We, as the collective aspect of the "Christ Mind" that split off, or, seemed to split off, became the "trans-temporal and transspatial Mind" that created the physical universe. And we created it in order to hide from God. Similar to a small child separating from his or her parents and going off to school, we felt fear and guilt over separating from God and Heaven. Projecting the psychology of our small egoic mind onto God, we imagined God to be angry with us and feared he would attack us for our transgression.

According to *The Disappearance of the Universe*, Yeshua was saying that *The Prodigal Son* was the story of Creation, not Genesis. The wrathful God of the Old Testament was the "projection of the divided Mind" of which we are all a part. As the collective Prodigal Son, we leave Heaven and travel to a foreign country (the physical universe). There we, like the Prodigal Son, "squander" the inheritance we received from our Father.

Rather than return to God and our home in Heaven, we allow our unconscious guilt to drive the dream of separation each time we incarnate. I say each time because I clearly had recollections of past lives which would be better called past dream dramas. (In *The Space Between Stars*, I explained the evidence that reincarnation was a belief held by the early Church Fathers but was taken out of the Bible for reasons not relevant to what we are exploring here.) And, when we wake up and leave this foreign land of this physical universe as the Prodigal Son did, we will find our loving Father ready to welcome us home. When we are born into a body, each of us is reexperiencing the original imagined separation.

Contemplating this view of creation, I was reminded of the Kabbalah's version of how the physical universe came into being. Here is the essence of what my Kabbalah teacher conveyed to me.

> In the beginning was the Endless Light which created a Vessel with which to share Its Light. After a while, the Vessel decided It was not content to simply receive but wanted to be able to share like Its Creator. The Vessel pushed back against the Light, and KABOOM! Like an immense cosmic thunderbolt, the Big Bang happened and the physical universe was born and the Vessel shattered into all the souls that would ever exist. The Light was now hidden behind the mask of the multiplicity of forms

making up the world of matter. Thus began the cosmic hide-and-seek game whereby all of us as souls instantly developed a dual nature. Containing the shards of the Vessel, we have the desire to receive and as sparks of the Light of the Creator, we have the desire to share. When we are born, we start the search for the Light. And, without knowing it, we are really seeking the Light in all the pleasures of the world. From chocolate and sex to worldly power and wealth, we are really seeking the bliss of the Light.

This story was similar to what I heard in *The Disappearance of the Universe*. The motive force behind the Big Bang and the creation of the physical universe of forms and bodies differed. Rather than guilt over mere thoughts of separation, the Kabbalah suggested a desire to be like the Creator. In the former story, we went into hiding. In the latter, the Light hid behind the mask of matter; it's the same effect but due to a different but related reason. In one, we seemed to separate when we wondered about being on our own apart from our Creator. Our own guilt and fear over even daydreaming about being on our own impelled us to create the physical universe as a place to hide. With the other, we separated from our Creator by pushing back to stop being like a child nursing at the breast of the Divine. Instead, we wanted to, in effect, grow up and be a giver like our Creator.

I felt the two stories were getting at a deeply buried truth about who we are and what motivates us. In both stories, we find ourselves in a physical universe that presents us with the challenge of pain and suffering while offering various passing pleasures. In either story, we find our way home while still in these bodies by seeking the Light. The Kabbalah teaches that we do this by learning to receive for the sake of sharing. While Yeshua teaches us we must forgive others for *only then* do we forgive ourselves.

Delving further into *The Disappearance of the Universe,* I was stunned to find a concept of mind that was startling yet familiar. Each time a baby is born, the original separation is reenacted. When we separated from God, or, believed we did, we experienced "three divisions of the mind." The first division involves a sense of self and other. "Twoness replaces oneness." We become aware of ourselves and of something else besides us, and we forget we were once at one with God. And, with the second division of the mind, we discover "two ways of interpreting what is going on."

Hadn't I experienced these divisions in that shamanic healing session I described in *The Space Between Stars,* the book I had just finished? Yes, it corresponded with what I had relived in that amazing session.

The session began with my lying comfortably on a soft mat while I breathed deeply with high-powered music playing in the background. I felt myself shift into an altered state of consciousness. As I lay there on a soft mat, I felt my consciousness rise out of my body. Suddenly, it was as if I were seeing the starry heavens as a shooting star would if a star had eyes. At first, I sped through space at such a rapid speed that the stars were a blur of streak lines. I suddenly slowed down to a near standstill, and I began moving in slow motion. I was floating in space as noiselessly and effortlessly as a helium-filled balloon being carried aloft by a gentle summer breeze. A framed doorway appeared. An earth-mother stood within it. She was a Native American wearing a beaded deer-skin vest and skirt. Her long ebony-colored hair glistened. Her face was welcoming and happy.

Another framed doorway appeared as I continued my journey through space. In this portal there stood a beautiful young woman with long chestnut-brown hair. She wore a full-length black skirt, high-buttoned black shoes, and a cream-colored high-collared blouse with long sleeves. Her arms were raised above her head while she attempted to pin up her long locks into an ample bun. Her hair style and apparel appeared to be Victorian. There was a slight resemblance to old sepia-colored photographs of my maternal grandmother.

Clearly, while speeding through space, I was experiencing the first division of the mind. I had no recollection of Heaven and the oneness. I was aware of being in a dualistic state of mind where I saw objects beyond myself: stars and portals with mother figures.

Not only was my memory of Heaven gone out of my awareness, I was not aware of any fear or guilt except by implication. Why was I in such a hurry? Why was I speeding so fast? It was as if I were taking flight from something I feared; its memory I had repressed.

Suddenly, I felt myself speed up. I was hurtling through space toward a distant doorway. It was empty and dark as though it was only a door frame suspended in the star-speckled darkness of space. No mother-figure was present in this one. I sped through it and came to an abrupt halt. At first, I felt encased in a small body. My tiny arms and hands were grasping for something to hold on to in order to feel some stability. I felt as if the tiny body were floating in a warm liquid. Without warning, I was overcome with fear. Every cell of this little body I was inhabiting was ablaze with fear of the burning, inescapable sensations of gnawing hunger.

A fear of starving to death threatened the existence of every cell as a brush fire gone out of control threatens all in its path. Every cell in this little flesh form was on fire with fear and the searing sensations of hunger. Somehow I sensed this fear dated back to the dawn of human history. Ancient. Primitive. Unrelenting. No relief was forthcoming. Finally, I stopped struggling and faced the fact that there was nowhere to go and nothing to do to escape.

At that very moment of surrender and acceptance, I felt a larger consciousness hovering above and to the right of this little body. As soon as I, as the consciousness encased in the little body, merged with the larger awareness, I felt relief. I felt free of the fear and hunger as I began to observe the overwhelming fear of the pain of starving to death. I was no longer threatened. My perspective shifted from being in the fire of fear and hunger to simply being still and watching the fear and hunger from above. I felt peaceful and calm once I, experiencing myself as the consciousness stuffed into the little form of flesh, merged with the spacious awareness of this transcendent consciousness.

The spaciousness of this awareness was both within and beyond the boundaries of the little body. I stopped identifying with the little body feeling fear and hunger. Minutes passed. Eventually, the gnawing pain of hunger abated, as if absorbed by this larger and calmer consciousness.

When I felt myself as split into two "seemingly" separate sets of consciousness, I was reexperiencing the second division of the mind. The smaller consciousness stuffed into the little flesh form of my fetal body is what *The Disappearance of the Universe* and *A Course in Miracles* call the ego; it is what I call the body-based sense of self. The larger and calmer consciousness was called the Holy Spirit: "God's inner link with His seemingly separated children." I called this consciousness my spirit in contrast to my soul which I see as the extension of my spirit which is housed in my body. I was also struck by the use of the word *seemingly*. It seemed to be God winking at me and confirming I was onto something. We only seem to be separate from God. Instead, the analogy is that we are safely asleep in bed while we dream we are in a dark jungle running from a large leopard. We have forgotten that we are still safe in bed no matter what danger we appear to be facing in the dream.

The third division of the mind occurred after this harrowing experience of hunger in the womb. At some point, most likely at the moment of my birth, I forgot about the quiet, calm, and comforting consciousness. I began identifying with the smaller, body-based sense of myself: my ego. This identification with my body along with my childhood experiences shaped my personal identity. In *The Space Between Stars*, I describe the moments in which I had a dim awareness of that larger consciousness, that higher self.

What is important is to wake up, as Eckhart Tolle said so succinctly in *The Power of Now*, from "the dream of matter, form, and separation." As I would discover, all that I was encountering was pointing me in the direction of waking up to a different understanding of reality. In this view of reality, spirit, and, its manifested form energy, came in first and matter, an illusory second. It was the reverse of the prevailing paradigm of scientific materialism in which matter rules. Recovering my vision was a spiritual issue and not a medical one.

Five

Unexpected Emissaries?

NOVEMBER 1, 2009

It was dusk and the flames of the fire were tickling the top of the fireplace. Sharon, a woman I had recently been introduced to by my friend Kerry, was reading aloud from a book about John of God. Sharon had been there. On this Sunday afternoon, one week before I was to depart for Brazil, Kerry and I were visiting with Sharon. We were seated on the sofa across from Sharon who was sitting on the base of the brick hearth. I felt a kind of tapping in the air above my head. I said to Sharon, "For the past ten minutes, something has been gently tapping on my energy field about a foot and a half over my head, and I feel I must acknowledge it." As soon as I spoke and called attention to the unseen presence, I felt a tingling shoot up my spine. Sensing something was there, I asked Sharon to look over my head and asked her to tell me if she could see anything.

"I see a woman with a featureless face of bluish-white light. She looks like a nun who is clothed in all white. Her hands are also a bluish-white light as they extend from her sleeves. There are no fingers, and she has a rosary draped over her right hand." Instantly, I saw the feminine figure clearly in my mind, and I could feel an intoxicating and dizzying excitement bubbling up in me like a fine champagne fizzing over the edges of a glass into which it has just been poured.

Turning to Kerry who was seated next to me, I asked her if she saw anything. "I see a female figure who looks like she is from Africa. Her skin is black and she is dressed in a black hooded cloak."

Nine days later, a few hours after I arrived in Abadiania, Brazil, I went with my friend Rod to the main hall of the Casa. It is where people gather before lining up to see John of God. A variety of pictures hung on the walls surrounding the chairs and benches. Rod took me to see a photograph of a famous Brazilian medium, the late Chico Xavier. He was leaning back and appeared to be in a trance. An apparition of St. Rita was touching his hand. She had a veil over her face as if her face were light and without features. A bouquet of roses was coming out of her sleeves and covered her hands.

In a DVD that introduces the Casa and the work of John of God entitled *I Do Not Heal, God Heals*, I learned that St. Rita was John of God's personal patron saint. I heard the story of how she appeared to John when he was sixteen years old and introduced him to his healing ministry. She told him to go to a nearby church where people were awaiting his arrival. He reported having no memory of what happened after he arrived at the church. A few hours passed. He remembered nothing except that people were thanking him for the healings that they had received. John had been unconscious while his body was used as a healing vehicle by unseen spirits. His mission as a healer-medium had begun.

After viewing the photograph of St. Rita's apparition, Rod took me to a small shop down the street from the Casa. He then showed me a diminutive statue of a black-faced female dressed in a hooded blue dress. "That's Our Lady Aparecida, the Brazilian Black Madonna," the shopkeeper said, and then went on to tell Rod and me the origin of the legend of Aparecida. The shopkeeper described what happened one day when some fishermen were dragging their nets in a river. Having little success that day, they prayed to the Blessed Mother to increase their catch. To their amazement, they saw that a statue of a Black Madonna had appeared in one of their nets. After the fishermen took her on board, they began to catch an abundance of fish. From then on she became known as Our Lady Aparecida which translates as Our

Lady Who Appeared.

Later, at dinner, I heard more about the Brazilian black Madonna. A man from California who was on his second trip to see John of God claimed, "It is said that she appeared because the black slaves were treated as if they were subhuman. With a Madonna that looked like them, the dark-skinned slaves had an opportunity to elevate their lowly status and feel better about themselves."

Still, I asked myself, *What was the significance of this unexpected appearance of two divine feminine figures? Why had the dark and light aspects of the archetypal feminine appeared to me? What did they have to do with my vision quest? What did I need to see?*

From my study of the psychology of Carl Jung, I saw Aparecida and St. Rita as two sides of one unifying energy. They embodied the light and dark (shadow side) of the archetypal feminine. Aparecida is an earth mother figure who embodies matter and the material world of form; whereas St. Rita, who had appeared with hands and a face of bluish-white light, represents spirit. Both body and spirit, the sensual and the spiritual, sex and love, need to be embraced, honored, and integrated in every man and woman if he or she is to achieve a state of inner wholeness and balance.

I had done a lot to attain this wholeness but the appearance of Our Lady Aparecida and St. Rita was the first sign that I needed to do more to transcend the split through the senses of my body and see there is no split between body (Aparecida) and spirit (St. Rita), between the sacred, the spiritual. In other words, I would later realize that the healing of my vision involved acquiring what *A Course in Miracles* calls "Christ vision." The light of the Divine Beloved shines through all forms of the material world: every tree, flower, rock, animal, and all of humankind. For as Christ said, "That which you do to the least among us, you do to me" (Matthew 25:24). And, in Saying Number 77 in *The Gospel of Thomas*, He said, "Split a piece of wood and I am there. Lift a stone and you will find me."

As I had written in *Love, Stress & Sex*, the split between love and sex was first identified by Freud over a century ago. The split involves a failure to achieve a union between love and sex, or, what Freud called the *affectionate* and the *sensual* currents. The man or woman suffering from this split is unable to feel sexual desire for the one he or she loves. Conversely, this same person is unable to feel love for the one whom he or she desires sexually, and, in fact, he or she often devalues, debases, and degrades the one desired. Freud called this inability of a man to feel love and sexual desire for one woman: the Madonna-whore complex. The woman unconsciously associated with the Madonna, often a wife, is revered but not desired sexually by the man with this complex; while the woman unconsciously equated with the whore, a mistress, is desired and not loved but is degraded.

This split between love and sex is still very much in evidence in the news and in my therapy practice; it appears in the form of internet pornography and widespread marital infidelity. In fact, at this very moment that I am writing this chapter, I just learned that a sex scandal involving a New York Congressman is in the news. This newly-married man was discovered to be displaying naked photos of himself via the internet to a female porn star and other women.

To me, this split between love and sex represents a more fundamental one in the human psyche: the split between body and spirit. Over the centuries, to be spiritual, one had to deny bodily desires and appetites. Sometimes, the spiritual seeker would seek to master the body by inflicting pain on it. But we are now at a point in human history where we can befriend the body as I was taught in the basic medical hypnosis course I took at Columbia University's College of Physicians and Surgeons when I was in training. Treating the body as one would a precious pet was used in helping patients quit smoking or stop overeating. The hypnotic suggestion went something like, "If a can of pet food with a label that reads EATING THIS IS DANGEROUS TO YOUR PET'S HEALTH, you would never feed it to your pet. You are just being asked to treat your body as you would your precious pet. Remind yourself, just as your pet needs your respect and protection so does your body."

Beyond treating our bodies better, we need to stop polluting and mistreating Mother Earth. While in Brazil, I would get a glimpse of the intimate connection between body and spirit. I knew that the energy of the light of spirit is what animates and gives the body life. Rather than just getting my body in shape as I did as an athlete, I began to see how focusing on sensing and feeling energy flowing through the body was necessary for my healing. As part of my first healing session at the Casa, I would have a direct experience of my spirit body, or what is called the etheric body. The appearance of these archetypal representations of the divine feminine foreshadowed what I needed to see and needed to change. In a little over a week, I would hear a beautiful recording of a woman singing *Ave Maria*, and I would feel the energy of an unseen supportive feminine presence open my heart just minutes before my first time in line to see John of God. . . .

II
Brazil & Beyond

When Jesus declares the light of the body is the eye, He certainly means that light depends upon mind, not upon the . . . lenses, muscles, the iris and pupil constituting the visual organism.
—Mary Baker Eddy, *Science & Health*

They [grievances] keep me in darkness and hide the light. Grievances and light do not go together but light and vision must be joined for me to see. To see I must lay grievances aside. I want to see and this will be the means by which I will succeed."
—Workbook Lesson 85 in *A Course in Miracles*

Sight, hearing or the spiritual senses of man are eternal. They cannot be lost.
—Mary Baker Eddy, *Science & Health*

Six

Yeshua—Not Jesus?

NOVEMBER 9, 2009

I WAS AWAKENED SHORTLY AFTER 2:00 A.M. AND felt the presence of three majestic beings hovering over my bed. In the darkness, I saw three silhouettes: their heads were touching the ceiling and their toes were pointing downward about a foot above my bed covers. I was reminded of Medieval oil paintings of levitating saints. From left to right, I sensed the first was Jesus, but could not tell who the other two were. *What a way to begin my first trip to Brazil*, I thought.

I softly called out, "Jesus?" There was no response. I called the name of Jesus two more times with no result. Then, something prompted me to say, "Yeshua?" Immediately I felt a flood of energy surge through me; it was similar to those times I was body-surfing and felt lifted and carried swiftly to shore by the swell of an ocean wave. Why had He responded to *Yeshua* but not *Jesus*? It wasn't until a few hours later when I was awakened by a rooster's crowing that I received an answer. . . .

Meanwhile, as I lay there staring into the darkness, the surge subsided. I puzzled for a few seconds, wondering, *Just who are these two other visitors hovering above me?* As my eyes grew more accustomed to the dark, I discerned that right above me was my host, the saint after whom the Casa was named: Dom Inacio de Loyola (St. Ignatius of Loyola); and next to him was San Francesco (St. Francis). Ever since my telephone consultations with Sophia, a woman from Milano, Italy, I had come to call him San Francesco in honor of his Italian heritage.

Yes you are, the syllables of the name Yeshua (Yes-hu-a) silently echoed in my mind and shape-shifted into these three words. *But what did they mean?* I wondered. From somewhere deep within, I heard a still, small voice say, "Yes you are divine, too. You are like me. You have the light of the Divine in you as does everyone, male and female, alike." Later, at breakfast, I shared with Rod and our Casa guide, Chris, how Jesus had appeared to me in the night, but did not respond when I softly said the name Jesus. Instead, He did answer by sending me a surge of energy when I said the name Yeshua. Before I could say another word, Rod and Chris reacted. Like a duet simultaneously singing the chorus of a song, they recited in unison the same refrain. They were both vociferous in stressing that the name Jesus is associated with centuries of organized religion, telling us we are sinners with little emphasis on our being created in the image of God.

Rod and Chris were in accord about the damage done in making human beings feel disconnected from the Divine. Therefore, they both concluded Yeshua's message was a much-needed one for the mass of humankind. As a step on my healing journey, it was something I needed to take in so that I could feel worthy and capable of receiving the blessings of restored vision, and, ultimately, the grace of true vision which, as I said earlier, is not simply seeing 20/20.

Walking to the Casa after breakfast, I had another curious play on syllables. I found it interesting that in Aramaic, the language spoken by Yeshua, the word ABBA is how He addressed God as Father. ABBA is an intimate version of father, something like daddy; and it struck me that the sound of ABBA and the sound of the name John can be heard in the correct Brazilian pronunciation of Abadiania (Abba-John-ia). In Brazilian Portuguese, the letter D is pronounced as a J. Certainly, a God we call ABBA would want us to know we are His Sons and Daughters, and, therefore, like Him. Eventually, it would become clearer to me that my being healed depended on my *believing* I was one of His beloved Sons.

Seven

No to Nerves?

NOVEMBER 10, 2009

"Don't ask for the regeneration of your optic nerves!" Rod, Chris, and I were just finishing dinner when Chris surprised me with this answer to my question. I had asked him how I should phrase my request for the healing of my vision. It is customary to go before John of God with a small piece of paper in hand on which are listed three requests written in Brazilian Portuguese. Chris was helping me refine my requests in English before translating them. Chris simply said, "Just ask for your sight to be restored. I recently took a woman with severed optic nerves before John of God, and her sight was restored. When her eye doctor examined her, he expected her nerves to be reconnected. Instead, he was amazed to find that her optic nerves were still severed, and yet, she was seeing perfectly."

A few days later, Rod purchased a book from the Casa store; it was entitled *The Book of Miracles: The Healing Work of Joao de Deus*. Rod read to me about the case of a young Brazilian woman who went blind after suffering from rheumatic fever, and later had her vision restored. The author, Josie RavenWing wrote: "The odd thing about her vision was that, according to the tests made by her ophthalmologist, there was absolutely no functioning of her optic nerves , and she should still have been blind." This woman, like the woman Chris mentioned, was also seeing perfectly without the functioning of the optic nerves, the key physical mechanism which enables us to see. On subsequent trips, I'd learn of two men who, like me, were legally blind. Both had their vision completely restored. One became a Casa guide. The other man was a physician who had had to give up his practice. After what is called an invisible surgery, which I'll explain later, he was able to resume his practice. The fascinating thing about the story of this physician was how and when I heard it. The sun had just dropped over the horizon. It was the end of my second trip to Abadiania in September 2010. Danielle, my traveling companion for that trip, and I were seated in the back of a taxi. We were only ten minutes from the airport in Brasilia. Dinah, a woman Danielle and I had seen at the Casa but did not know, had hitched a ride with us to the airport. Dinah was seated in the front. There was a lull in the conversation. Looking out the window, I had the thought, *I've enjoyed my time at the Casa but I don't think I'll be coming back. I don't think this is where my vision will be restored.* The instant I finished my thought, Dinah spun around and told me the story of a legally-blind physician. "I remember how overjoyed he was. He had tears in his eyes, and he cried out, 'I can see! I can see!'" I told Dinah that I was legally blind. To which she responded, "I didn't know that. I'm getting the feeling you are supposed to come back to the Casa." Given the timing of her story, I agreed. I'd be coming back. It was as if an angel spoke through her, silencing my unspoken doubts.

On my third trip in May of 2012, I would hear of a man who was completely blind having his vision restored; and, on my fourth trip, I'd be in the main hall of the Casa on the afternoon of All Hallow's Eve (Halloween). Right in front of my damaged eyes, I'd see a man suddenly overjoyed, and I'd hear a Casa guide call out, "A man who has been blind from birth is now able to see for the first time!"

At first, I was stunned. *But then was this really such a surprise? Hadn't Rod told me of an ancient saying, 'The Philosopher's Stone (the symbol of the personal truth each of us seeks) lies in the middle of the road, and the carts of men roll over it? Hadn't the road to Brazil been paved with mortar mixed with the concrete of one message—reinforced by being repeated in various forms from varied sources? And, what's that one message? My body's eyes did not need to be healed for my vision to be restored! Hadn't I received all those messages regarding physical reality being like a dream, an illusion? I loved the way the spiritual teacher Drunvalo Melchizedek said in an interview on YouTube, "Life is not what it seems, not even close to what most of our parents believed to be true. We live in a dream that our mind has crystallized into what we call reality. We believe it is fixed and can only be changed according to the laws of physics. The Maya believe you will soon know a part of yourself that is so ancient that it goes beyond the stars and planets as fixed worlds. They are just a dream also, and, like a dream upon wakening, you realize it was nothing but light, or, better still, nothing but pure consciousness."* I was thinking of all the messages I'd been receiving regarding the illusory nature of physical reality.

The first message had come in the form of the final episode of the TV series *Life on Mars*. The whole gritty police drama had been a dream. Then, the next form the message took came from *The Disappearance of the Universe*—all healing is of the mind which creates the world we see. Later, I'd hear Eckhart Tolle pull together the various forms of the message in the following passage from his audio book *The Power of Now*.

> What you perceive as a dense physical structure called the body, which is subject to disease, old age, and death, is not ultimately real, is not you. It is a misperception of your essential reality, which is beyond birth and death, and is due to the limitations of your mind, which, having lost touch with being, creates the body as evidence of its illusory belief in separation and to justify its state of fear.

This really struck me since I had been told I would see clearly again when I could see through the eyes of God with total love and no fear. And, what were the eyes of God, but the eyes of my spirit, my consciousness.

On another audio book, *The Autobiography of a Yogi*, the life story of the Indian saint, Paramahansa Yogananda, I'd hear words that were remarkably similar to those of Eckhart Tolle, "The body is literally manufactured and sustained by mind." Then, there was my discovery of Mary Baker Eddy's *Science & Health* at the Whole Health Expo in Boston. The book's message took the form: heal the mind so it sees the truth, and heal physical disease instantly.

Throughout the text and the workbook lessons of *A Course in Miracles*, I'd hear how true vision is not with the body's eyes. And, then, the door to my mind was blown off its hinges with the force of the wind that blew open the door to Scrooge's apartment as the ghost of Jacob Marley entered, wielding chains. This describes the mind-blowing impact that the following comment made by Eckhart Tolle in *The Power of Now* had on me. It puts my healing quest into the wider context of the next stage in the evolution of human consciousness. Wow! I feel so grateful for the guidance that keeps coming my way.

> The time-bound mode of consciousness is deeply embedded in the human psyche. But what we are doing here is part of a profound transformation taking place in the collective consciousness of the planet and beyond, the awakening of consciousness from the *dream of matter, form, and separation,* the ending of time. [Italics added] We are breaking mind patterns that have dominated human life for aeons, mind patterns that have created unimaginable suffering on a vast scale.

It was a sunny August afternoon in the Adirondacks when I heard Eckhart Tolle speak these words with his calm, soothing voice. I was staying at my friend's vacation home. In three months, I'd be leaving for Brazil. And, on the day after I arrived, I'd have my heart opened by two visions. These visions depicted the suffering I had caused as a result of my task-oriented, time-driven Type A personality. I was clearly identified with the "time-bound mode of consciousness."

The initial vision was of a small canvas an artist could use to paint a picture. The top two-thirds of which were maroon-colored which I soon realized was dried blood and not paint. The bottom third was a fresh bright white with three bright red streams of blood dripping down the clean white surface. I received the message that this was my contribution to the blood spilled centuries ago in one of the darkest periods in human history. This vision was followed by the little canvas expanding into a large one. The message was that this canvas represented the massive amount of blood produced by all who participated in the slaughter and "unimaginable suffering" of so many innocents. . . .

Eight

A Contrite Knight

NOVEMBER 11, 2009

"Who was this impressive man with dark, fierce, penetrating eyes, a full gray beard, and a small black hat?" I asked my friend Rod. I reasoned that he might be able to identify this unknown priest since Rod was an Episcopal priest as well as a seasoned traveler to the Casa (this was his fourth trip). I told Rod how the man looked like the Greek Orthodox priests I had seen on the island of Mykonos at Easter. He answered my question by taking me to the main hall of the Casa where, as I mentioned earlier, people gather before lining up to see John of God. Rod pointed to a large framed black-and-white picture. I was speechless. There, before me, was the priest. It was none other than King Solomon.

The vision of King Solomon came to me the first time I was having what is called a crystal bath. Actually, the bath is not of water but light delivered while one is lying on a bed with a cloth draped over the eyes. Above the bed, seven lights are positioned on adjustable metal arms so that, depending on one's height, each light can be lined up with each of the body's seven energy centers known as chakras. I won't go into the chakra system except to say that optimal health occurs when the chakras are balanced and the unseen energy vortex of each chakra is spinning freely. (You can easily familiarize yourself with chakras by googling CHAKRAS on the internet.) Each of the seven light bulbs shines through a crystal mined from the crystal caves under the earth beneath the Casa.

Crystals are known as wonderful transmitters and amplifiers of energy so that the Casa is said to be one of our planet's sacred energy vortices. Again, in order to keep the focus on my healing quest, I leave it up to you, the reader, to research the concept of energy medicine and sacred energy vortices.

As I lay there staring into those fiercely-focused dark eyes, I witnessed the face of King Solomon fading after what seemed to be approximately one minute of the forty minutes I lay under the lighted crystals. Crystal-bath sessions range from a twenty-minute minimum to a maximum of an hour. I would find that it would take twenty minutes or more before I began to have any visions; it took that long for me to enter the kind of altered state of consciousness conducive to having visions. A new face appeared. It was the face of a Spanish nobleman or cleric, looking up to his left, my right. He, too, had on a small black hat. He appeared arrogant and haughty to me. Right after that, Rod helped me identify King Solomon. Then Rod pointed to another black-and-white picture of a man. "Is this the man you saw?" Rod asked. It was. Before us was a picture of Dom Inacio; only he seemed compassionate and reverent, not haughty. Why had both King Solomon and Dom Inacio appeared to me as so fiercely masculine? The answer lay in the next vision. . . .

Who is this knight I see in chain mail, not armor, his helmet in hand, kneeling on one knee, his right one, his back to an old rugged wooden cross, its thick shaft and arms weathered and gray? As I lay there wondering who it was, I suddenly realized: *Why it's me from another century!* I was filled with a heart-searing contrition over my part in the Crusades. Yes, the word was *contrition*. I felt contrite over my contribution to the bloodshed caused by the Crusades in battle after bloody battle. The word contrition was not one I tended to use; it was something of which I had a dim recollection. I recalled the phrase, an act of contrition. I associated it with Catholicism; however, I was raised Episcopalian so the word contrition was not in my religious vocabulary. Still, it's exactly what I felt. I vaguely recalled from Catholic friends the phrase, "I am heartily sorry." I was heartily sorry for my part in the Crusades.

In an instant, I tearfully forgave myself with a flash of reasoning that, like a lightning bolt, seemed to come from beyond me: *I forgive myself because I loved my religious tradition. What I did, I did out of love even though, now, in retrospect, I can clearly see that I was misguided.*

I left the crystal bath slightly dazed . . . I was still that knight. With tears in my eyes, I got in line to go before John of God for the first time. As I entered through the doorway to the Casa, I saw, through my tears, an old rugged wooden cross to my right. It resembled the one in my vision. The recording of a woman singing *Ave Maria* acted as a lever, prying open my heart even more than it already was. Her soft, soprano voice opened the way for a new flood of tears: I suddenly saw how a crusader attitude was still operating in my current life. It took the form of the task-oriented Type A personality, the very attitude that had led to my athletic and academic achievements. What saddened me was how this crusader attitude had caused me to be impatient with each of the women I had loved as a romantic partner from my college days to the present. I now felt badly, and yet, at the same time, I felt good because I felt cleansed; it was as if my heart became a bucket that I was tipping over and emptying of the sewage caused by my continuing crusader attitude. In an upcoming chapter, I'll share the startling story Chris confided to me when I told him of my vision of myself as a contrite crusader. It was not common knowledge, but was known only by those few, comprising the core of the Casa. . . .

Now, looking back, I can see how I had been out of balance. The realm of time and mind was where I had dwelled. I had been caught up in doing and accomplishing with the exception of brief periods during daily meditation. How else does anyone get through graduate school to receive a doctorate except by exercising the mind?

I had developed the qualities associated with the mind: thinking, analyzing, problem-solving. I had developed the mental tendency to honor time by doing things quickly and efficiently. The merciless tendency to be impatient accompanied my efforts as a graduate student and later as a professional. These qualities associated with the archetypal masculine all aimed to *doing* something. And, in my work as a psychologist, what was my major *doing*? It was identifying and solving mental and emotional problems. I had devoted my life to being a professional problem-solver. I would come to learn that a feminine consciousness contained the ultimate solution to the problems faced by human beings. It involved an emphasis on an all-inclusive and unconditional acceptance of others and their problems. *Being* is the essence of this feminine consciousness, not *doing*. It is an ever-alert *actionless awareness.*

To illustrate this kind of expansive, non-judgmental, and all-accepting *being* consciousness, I find myself thinking of three of the poems of Shabkar, an 18th century Tibetan Buddhist Master:

> In the vastness of the sky
> Without center or edges,
> The sun shines, illuminating
> All things without choosing.
> This is the way you should help all beings.

Shabkar continues to describe this expansive, ever-alert *actionless awareness* that is open to all perspectives.

> One must remain in the vastness
> Alert and lucid,
> Letting one's gaze encompass
> The infinity of the sky,
> As though seated on the summit,
> Of a mountain open to all the horizons.

Shabkar's next poem reveals the timeless, eternal quality of this expansive state of consciousness, our timeless true self.

> Sky empty and luminous
> Beyond all attachments,
> Remains.
> Me, the setting sun
> Resplendent with light,
> Will not remain at all.
> I pass behind the western summit
> To reappear again soon
> Above the mountains of the East.

The sun is likened to what I call our body-based sense of self. This is the little self, the embodied soul, caught in the cycle of time, of birth and death. Like the sun's settings and risings, the little self, the embodied soul, keeps disappearing and reappearing. This was my crusader self in contrast to my timeless, true nature. It would be at the end of my fourth trip to the Casa in October 2012, that I'd get the impression that the crusader cycle was over.

While I was in a crystal bath session on a sunny Saturday afternoon, I had a vision with three parts to it. At first, I saw a medallion, its metal covered with a greenish-tinged patina. The cameo profile of a knight, wearing his helmet with the visor closed, was etched into the metal. Instantly, I received the message that I had been this knight, now represented on this metal, turned green with the passing of the ages.

Above and to the left of me as this helmeted knight, appeared another medallion. On its greenish metal was the head of a queen, facing forward and slightly to the right. I received the message that this was an image of Queen Isabella of Spain. I was startled to notice that her eyes seemed alive; I felt a little uneasy as she peered down menacingly at me as this knight.

Queen Isabella disappeared. In the space up and to the right of me as this knight, I saw a medallion of another Queen. Her cameo profile faced to the left as mine did. The message I received was that this was an image of Queen Elizabeth of England. Evidently, I had served Spain in one lifetime, and England in the next. First, I was on one side, then on the other. This was not new to me; I had seen this switching sides in a vision I'd had in a crystal bath session on my third trip to the Casa in September 2010. I saw myself as a bare-chested Native American brave on horseback, the leather strap of his quiver, containing razor-sharp arrows, across his chest, his bow in one hand, the reins in the other. I received the message that he was a member of the Wolf Clan, and he was hunting. To my left, a U.S. Cavalry soldier, lay wounded in a ditch, his blue battle-worn uniform, torn and tattered from hand-to-hand combat. The message I received was that he and his troop wiped out the Wolf Clan. In an instant, it came to me that after a lifetime as the Wolf Clan brave, I had a lifetime as this soldier. I had been on both sides of the conflict. Then, the brave and soldier disappeared.

Immediately, to my right, I had a vision of a divine feminine figure. I recognized her from paintings I had seen. She was Quan Yin, an Asian goddess; her name literally translates as "one who hears the cries of the world." She is known for her all-embracing love and omnipresent compassion. She was looking upwards, her body vibrating as if she were a rocket ready to launch. She was preparing to ascend. Her long black hair was shaped into two ample buns, one over each of her ears, as if she were wearing a set of head phones. I found myself thinking of Carrie Fisher as Princess Leia in *Star Wars*. In particular, I recalled Princess Leia, appearing in an endlessly-looping holographic image, making her plea for help against the onslaught of the Death Star Troopers of the evil Empire: "Obi-Wan Kenobi, you're our only hope . . ."

Perhaps there was something to my random association to Princess Leia and *Star Wars*. I suddenly realized that Quan Yin was presenting an important symbolic message to me: it was time to *ascend* and thereby *transcend* the endless cycle of action and reaction, a deadly centuries-old cycle that had led to one warring conflict after another. She was conveying to me it was time to ascend to the higher level of consciousness which recognizes the sacred oneness of all life on Earth and beyond.

I had the intuition that these visions of myself as a knight, brave, and soldier were just a glimpse of the many lifetimes as some kind of warrior. I had the feeling that I had gone back and forth over the centuries. It seemed that I had been given the opportunity to experience both sides of many long-standing conflicts. Contemplating the aged greenish metal of the knight medallion, I had a feeling of finality. The resplendent sun of my knight-crusader self had set, never to dawn again.

My sense of myself was shifting from contrite knight-crusader or compassionate warrior to a sense of my timeless true nature: Shabkar's empty and luminous sky, beyond all attachments. It was becoming clear that learning to fully identify with my timeless true nature held the key to my healing.

Nine

Ramrod Revision?

NOVEMBER 17, 2009

STEEL RODS RAMMED THROUGH THE CENTER OF my back? I groaned and cried out, more with shock than pain. There was some discomfort. I was afraid my groans might wake Rod who was sleeping in the next room. But as loud as I sounded to myself, I was not using my vocal chords. Why? Because, I looked down to my right and saw the silhouette of my physical body lying in bed.

Here was that theme again: the physical was not so important in healing. I was fully aware as my body lay there lifeless with not even the slightest movement and no sign of breathing. And yet, here I was in a transparent body of light which was shaped like my physical body. I later learned that this energy or spirit body is often referred to in the literature on spiritual healing. It is called the etheric body or etheric double. The latter term is used since the etheric body is, in effect, a subtle energy body that matches the contours of one's physical body. Within this energy body and without the involvement of my physical body, I was still able to experience some of my senses: I could see without physical eyes, hear without ears, and feel the touch of unseen hands lifting my etheric body. I could also feel my legs of light bending over the side of the bed, while my feet of light were flat on the floor. I had never had a spiritual experience like this before! . . .

I was stunned by this experience of being lifted up and having steel rods rammed into, and, seconds later, forcefully retracted from, the back of this etheric body of light. This was the first part of what happened on the night I did my revision ritual in preparation for my stitches to be removed. However, my stitches were invisible since I'd had an invisible surgery a week earlier. What is an invisible surgery? Before I answer, unless you're Brazilian, which means you are quite familiar with what I am about to say, you may want to brace yourself, take a deep breath, fasten your seat belt, and get mentally and emotionally prepared for take off into an unfamiliar firmament. An invisible surgery is essentially a spiritual or energy surgery performed by—remember my mentioning my feeling lifted by unseen hands—what is known at the Casa as the entities of light. Entities? Some of these unseen beings are saints who are no longer in physical form. Dom Inacio and San Francesco are two such saints. Other entities were physicians when they were alive; and now they make themselves available to come through the medium John of God to help those in need of healing. Two such examples are Dr. Almeida and Dr. Cruz. Last I heard there are said to be thirty-three entities that come, or, as the Brazilians call it, incorporate in John of God and work through him. There are many others who operate independently and work on individuals directly without going through John of God's body. They do, however, utilize the sacred space opened by John of God and other mediums seated in two rows on either side of the aisle leading to the chair in which John of God is seated to receive those seeking healing. The entities work on all levels: physical, mental, emotional, and spiritual.

Regarding the aforementioned Brazilian woman who could see after a series of invisible surgeries despite her non-functioning optic nerves, Josie RavenWing wrote this about the entities in her book, *The Book of Miracles*: "Did they somehow rewire her brain? Or, did they create an entirely new way for her to be able to perceive this world? This is one of the many mysteries of their work." She also had this to say about the entities:

> Of all that I have heard or experienced at the Casa, the entities always work on the source of the problem. That source may be

mental, emotional, physical or spiritual, or a combination of any of these elements, although I have been told by the volunteer staff of the Casa that the entities say that from their perspective, the source is almost always spiritual. And because the entities work on the source, true healing takes place, not just the curing of symptoms.

Like the Brazilian woman and the legally blind physician both of whom had a series of invisible surgeries, I had just begun my own series. A group of us entered the Casa and were directed to the room where the entities perform the invisible surgeries. While the Casa is ecumenical and is open to all faiths, it has a Roman Catholic air, the exterior being painted blue and white in honor of Mother Mary. The interior of the Casa resembles the inside of a Catholic church. As the group of us seeking surgery entered the Casa, we walked past wooden pews filled with others seeking healing. They sat shoulder to shoulder. Sitting in any of the three rooms that lead to the surgery room is called "sitting in current." The current is the healing energy generated by the entities and all who sit there in hopes of being healed.

Once our surgery group entered the door to the surgery room, we also sat next to each other on wooden pews. I would estimate that there were approximately thirty of us seated there. Soft music was playing, and a young woman led us in a guided meditation, preparing us to receive the entities.

This lovely woman began in Brazilian Portuguese for a few lines and then shifted to English, addressing each of us, she said, "Place your right hand over your heart. The entities are now beginning to work on you." She continued to alternate between Brazilian Portuguese and English. "Picture that Jesus and Mother Mary are here with you. Feel their love as the entities perform the invisible surgery."

I felt a surge of exhilarating energy up my spine, followed by flutters of energy in my eyes as well as in and around my heart. Moments later, I felt flutters of energy up my nostrils. I would later learn from Chris that this was the energy equivalent of the forceps used by John of God in visible surgeries. According to Chris, the forceps are being used to remove the blocks in the energy flow that should be moving freely between the right and left hemispheres of the brain by way of the corpus callosum, the area of tissue connecting the two. Restoring the flow helps to balance the masculine and feminine energies which have been so out of balance in both men and women for centuries. This balance was to be a focus for healing that I'd encounter on all my trips to the Casa. It would also come up the night of my revision ritual. It helped explain the rods rammed into either side of the spine of my etheric body, midway up my back. So that when the rods came through they were inches from where my heart would be in my physical body. It seemed that the rods were to open up what in yoga is called the *ida* and *pingdala*, the channels in which male and female energies flow.

Immediately after the entities extracted the rods, the entities encircled the head of my etheric body with a thin metal band, approximately one inch wide. It extended from my forehead just above where my eyes would be and just above where my ears would be, and around the back of my head. Another metal band was placed over the center of my head from side to side, connecting to the first band where each ear would be. Then a third band was placed over the center of my head from the center of my forehead to the center of the back of my head, intersecting the other bands. These intersecting bands formed a quadrant or cross which reminded me of a skull cap, resembling a helmet or crown of some sort. I felt the entities press on the bands. I saw a flash of green light. I asked them to please remove my glaucoma; I felt them press again on metal bands and I saw another flash of light.

The entities then began to lay me back down into my physical body. A shiver shot up my spine as I felt the back of my etheric body being touched. I saw three sets of bronze-colored hands gently stroking the back of my etheric body of light. Reflecting back on it, I found it fascinating that I could see not only in front of me as I would be able to do if I were looking through the eyes of my physical body. But I could also see the hands on the back of my etheric body as if I were looking on from behind my back. The same held true for seeing the flash of green light both from what would be the perspective of my physical eyes as well as from above my head looking down and also from the side.

After I was reunited with my physical body, I lay there thinking of how I had heard that the entities may announce their presence by rattling something such as a window or door. Right then, after I had this thought, the fork on the plate by my bed rattled. It was the plate on which Rod had brought me a piece of watermelon. I had cleaned it and placed it there for the entities to announce their arrival. I smiled as I thought, *The entities have a sense of humor—they announced their exit instead.*

Seeing, hearing, and feeling without the use of my physical body? Wasn't this the consistent message that kept coming through in various forms? Spirit is primary. Matter is secondary. Now I had experienced this for myself. Two days after arriving home, I had a confirmation of my experience. I just happened to turn on the television, and I heard a minister claiming that it is not with the senses of the physical body with which we see, hear, touch, taste, and smell. "It is the *spirit man* that experiences through the senses of the body." Yes! It is our invisible etheric energy body, or, call it what you will, soul or spirit or consciousness, that experiences the visible, material world through our physical body, or, as I like to call it, our *soul suit* or our *corporeal costume.*

A few days later, I had a vision which further challenged the substantiality of matter, of the physical. It was shortly after sunset. Rod and I were seated in the main hall of the Casa along with other visitors to the Casa and a group of nuns who unfailingly gather every night, all 365 nights a year, to say the rosary. Speaking in the beautifully lyrical language of Brazilian Portuguese, the nuns began with some prayers. Once the nuns took up their rosary beads, I knew the repeating of the rosary was underway. As soon as they began, I had a vision of three tiny orbs of green light, forming a horizontal line. It was as if I were viewing the orbs on the screen of a small TV monitor located in the middle of my forehead slightly above my eyes. This is an area known in spiritual circles as the third eye which is associated with spiritual vision. This area is also known as the sixth chakra which is thought to be a seat of wisdom and insight. It is where I had seen all my visions I had had during my crystal bath sessions. The little orbs possessed an aliveness as they appeared to be vibrating as though readying themselves for lift off like tiny helicopters. Suddenly, they did lift off and began orbiting each other as subatomic particles in an atom. Then, they coalesced into one larger green orb and flew from the screen and penetrated into the flesh of my forehead. My head swayed back slightly.

Many minutes passed and before the nuns finished saying the rosary, I had an exact repetition of this vision of the three adorable orbs of green light so vibrant with life.

I turned to Rod and asked him if he could tell what the nuns had said at the beginning of the rosary and at the end. Rod's response made sense of my experience: "In the beginning, they were probably saying, 'In the name of the Father, Son, and Holy Spirit.' And, at the end, they were probably saying, 'Glory be to the Father, Son, and Holy Spirit.'"

Wow! Had I been given a glimpse of the spiritual basis of the physical universe? What was I being shown about the Holy Trinity? Was it that the three-in-one spirit is what infuses the subatomic particles at the basis of the material—proton, electron, and neutron—world with life?

It seemed I was being called to awaken from what Eckhart Tolle referred to as the dream of identifying with matter, form, and the idea that we are separate little selves. I was being called to awaken from the story of the little me, the embodied soul, whether it was the story of my current lifetime or a past one. It was being revealed that past lives were better understood as past dream dramas. The entities were revealing that we are much more than our physical bodies. We are not mere meat stuffed into the casing of our soul suit; we are not separate sausage links, passively strung up in an old-fashioned butcher's shop. We are these etheric energy bodies of light that animate our physical forms. Who we are transcends time and space, and true vision extends beyond the body. . . .

Ten

Thunderbolt to the Stars?

NOVEMBER 20, 2009

I SAW A FLASH OF LIGHTNING AND HEARD A simultaneous crack of thunder. I was stretched out on a massage table in a small room adjacent to the living room in Chris's cottage. It had begun to drizzle. I had just left the Casa where I'd said good-bye and thanked John of God. The rain picked up right outside the gate to Chris's cottage; I stopped by to thank him before going off to meet Rod for our last dinner. We were flying home tomorrow. The thunderbolt happened seconds after I'd said a prayer in which I'd called on the entities to bless Chris for all he had done for me and so many others over his years as a guide at the Casa.

Immediately following the thunderbolt, Chris fell back onto the large pillowy cushions next to the massage table where I lay. He had a huge smile on his face, exclaiming, "Phew, what a feeling of power!" He seemed to have received his blessing. Suddenly, I saw a shaft of golden-white light shoot up before me. It extended from the table up to the ceiling, forming a rectangular corridor of light. I watched a paper-thin, golden body of light rise up out of me. Like a cut-out of a featureless paper doll, this golden-white light body floated up to and then through the ceiling. The next thing I knew, I was looking at a distant nebula with its cluster of stars and cloud of star dust set against the backdrop of the dark depths of outer space. Later on, it would be revealed to me that I was actually seeing Andromeda, the neighboring galaxy to our Milky Way.

To my surprise, I had the word, *Home*, enter my thoughts. In the blink of an eye, I was aboard a spacecraft, observing golden-light beings with the light appearing to be condensed into thin rope-like bodies. Their glistening golden hairless heads resembled metallic, almost helmet-like, skull caps. A group of four or five of them looked like a team of physicians; they were leaning over the golden-light body that had floated out of my physical body. One of them held a set of instruments that appeared to be made of gold. I could see this being was operating on the body of light.

A female being appeared to the far left of the operating team. How did I know she was female? It was her eyes. It's almost as if she had long lashes, framing beautiful eyes which emanated a sweet feminine quality. She motioned to me with an oustretched arm and then she shifted her gaze as she pointed toward a male golden-light being. Somehow I knew this being was me. I watched as she embraced this version of me. We wrapped our rope-like bodies as if we were easily bendable pipe cleaners. We intertwined into the shape of the medical symbol of a caduceus. Our eyes emitted a loving energy as our heads faced each other. There were erotic feelings coursing through both of our bodies. I was surprised to experience sexual feelings similar to what human beings feel. It was astonishing to be as turned on as I was without the feeling of flesh pressed against flesh and without the female body parts associated with human sexuality. No breasts. No shapely buttocks. No merging of male and female genitalia.

The whole scene faded and I was once again seeing the interior of Chris's cottage. With what had I seen all this that had happened? Was it with my mind's eye? My consciousness? My spirit? My etheric body?

With what was I seeing when I saw without my body's eyes as I looked at my body lying in bed during my revision? Wasn't I seeing with that by which the eyes see but cannot be itself seen by the eyes? I was seeing myself looking out of another pair of eyes set in the head I had as a golden light being. I found myself thinking of those words from the ancient Hindu text of *The Upanishads*: *What cannot be seen with the eyes but that whereby the eye can see, know this alone is Brahmin, the Spirit, and not what people here [on Earth] adore."*

While I was watching the golden-light body float to the ceiling, I was looking through my body's eyes. But once I was aware of being in the night sky of outer space or on the spaceship, I had not been able to discern any form of body and eyes with which to see. Nonetheless, I was seeing clearly. I then wondered, *How do any of us see in dreams? Our body's eyes are closed. Also, with what was I feeling those erotic feelings while I was watching myself as a golden-light being intertwined in an erotic union with a female golden-light being.* Just days ago, I had seen, felt, and heard while my physical body lay asleep. *How was I seeing, feeling, and hearing without my body's eyes, flesh, and ears during my first revision? And, how was I feeling turned on in the golden-light body while I was watching the union from approximately ten feet away and while I was simply an invisible awareness and not in any kind of body?*

After I told Chris what I had experienced, he told me about the concept of star seeds, and how it had been revealed to him that I was one. Chris explained that approximately 11,000 years ago, souls who had had lifetimes in other dimensions as star beings incarnated on Earth, that is, had *seeded* on Earth with the mission to help humanity evolve spiritually. However, the star seeds had gotten caught up in the various wars and especially the Crusades. Mired in religious conflicts, the star seeds had lost their way. Chris said that one of his unofficial missions at the Casa was to help star seeds get back on track so that they could help the great shift in consciousness taking place on Earth. Following my vision of myself as a knight, Chris told me, "You are so plugged into the Casa. So many of you who have had past lives in the Crusades are showing up here at the Casa for healing." Chris then went on to say, "Only a few of the core staff at the Casa know this. John of God was said to have been a pope during the Crusades; as such, he is to be a vehicle for healing 9 million people (during my trip in May of 2012, I heard it said that thus far 8 million people had received healing) in order to expiate the pain and suffering he set in motion by exercising his religious authority." I did not check this out with others at the Casa, but it seemed to make sense with what I had experienced.

Obviously, getting back to star seeds, coming from different star systems such the Pleiades, Arcturus, Orion, or Sirius, star beings could not be carbon-based life forms as human beings are. If they were carbon-based life form, star beings would be incinerated. I told Chris that it was in my time with the Maya in Mexico and Guatemala when I discovered I'd had lifetimes as a Pleiadian. I also told Chris how I had confirmation of my having Pleiadian roots and a synchronicity, suggesting I'd had lifetimes as an Andromedan. This information came to me during a workshop at the National Hypnotherapy convention in Nashua, New Hampshire, that took place in August of 1996.

Workshop participants paired off and each member of the pair took turns focusing on the space above the head of the other. We were to look for each other's higher self or spirit guide and report what we saw. Above the head of the man with whom I was paired, I saw an image of an angel like angels I had seen in Medieval paintings. My partner reported seeing a slender light being with a large oval head and almond-shaped eyes. He also saw the word Andromeda. At that time, I was not aware that Andromeda is the neighboring galaxy to those of us on planet Earth whose galaxy is the Milky Way. That night, when I arrived back at my home in Connecticut, Don, the man renting a room from me was watching a movie. "Hi, Don, what are you watching?" I asked. "*The Andromeda Strain*," he answered.

Flashing ahead to a few months after I returned home from Brazil, I contacted Marilynn Hughes, an author I had heard speaking on the late-night radio show, *Coast to Coast*. I had heard Marilynn say something that satisfied the egalitarian, Jacksonian Democrat in me, the one who believes all men are created equal. "We are all spiritual beings but some of us have *chosen* to be galactic beings, having lifetimes in other star systems and other galaxies." So it wasn't an elitist issue; it was simply a matter of choice.

When I emailed Marilynn with a description of the golden-light beings with rope-like bodies, I asked her if she recognized who they might be. She believed them to be Andromedan.

While all this was fascinating, I felt that what I was being led to see was not the ultimate answer to my vision quest. Yes, it resonated with me that I had had some connection with the starry heavens. As a child, I had asked myself, *Where would I be if I had never been born?* Each time, I asked, I would get a picture of the starry heavens. There was the same sense of home I had felt, looking at the distant nebula that I later learned was the galaxy of Andromeda. But there was something else here. Past lives as a crusader, or as a soldier, and lifetimes as a star being were still relegating my sense of self to some form- or body-based identity. Even as elevated as it seemed to be inhabiting a less material form as an Andromedan with a thin, rope-like body of golden light, it was still a physical form. I was beginning to sense something in me was seeing without my body's eyes. This something was limitless and not limited by the contours of my current body or any body I had had in a past life on Earth or elsewhere. It was formless in contrast to form, infinite in contrast to finite; and I could hear that distinctive voice of Rod Serling, echoing in my memory one of his weekly introductions to the 1960s TV series, *The Twilight Zone*:

There is a fifth dimension beyond that which is known to man. It is as vast as space and as timeless as infinity. It is the middle ground between light and shadow, between science and superstition, and it lies between the pit of man's fears and the summit of his knowledge. This is the dimension of imagination. It is an area which we call the Twilight Zone.

It would be in September of 2010, my next trip to this quaint village of Abadiania—where the veil separating the world of matter and the world of spirit is thinner than it is in other places—that I'd have an eye-opening experience in the crystal bath . . . one that would suggest my true identity and true source of my sight, and, actually, the true identity of and true source of sight for each one of us is as vast as the starry heavens of outer space. . . .

Eleven

The Void?

SEPTEMBER 11, 2010

"What is the void? It is often mentioned in this book I'm reading." Danielle, my traveling companion on this trip, asked about this concept of the void just moments after Ann, a woman from Germany, had brought it up while Danielle was still in line at the breakfast buffet. Without any hesitation, I told her what I knew from my readings. I told her that it was the black emptiness out of which all in existence emerges and returns. I compared it to outer space with no light, no stars or planets. The instant I said it was black, I thought, *Is it really black or does it have to be?* I kept that to myself. I didn't want to confuse Danielle to whom the whole concept was new so I stayed with what I had heard and read even though I had just had a very peaceful experience of the comforting black depth of the void in my most recent crystal bath.

While I lay there staring into the darkness, I felt as if I were in some vast cave-like womb which was completely enveloping me. In contrast, a few years earlier I had a vision of what the Kabbalah called the Endless Light. I awoke to a vision of the curtains parting in my bedroom. Through the large triple-paned window, I saw wave upon wave of golden-white light billowing forth, forming an endless rolling sea. Two days after describing the void as black, I was lying there in my next crystal bath when I had a vision of a pure white void. Instead of feeling comforted as I had by the black void, I felt contained and enlivened by the all-encompassing void of white light. I was then reminded of my struggle to reconcile the idea of ultimate reality being depicted as the light of love and the black emptiness of the void. I described it in *A Matter of Love*:

> Ultimately, the forms of things are arising from the creative emptiness of what physics calls the field and the mystics call the void. The void is the ultimate creative emptiness, the underlying reality and oneness from which all phenomena arise and pass away. I had heard of how mystics found such indescribable peace in experiencing this ultimate emptiness. At first, I was not able to reconcile this concept of emptiness with my spiritual experiences that revealed how love is the underlying reality.

I found myself reflecting on that moment when Sharon had a vision of what I later realized was St. Rita over my head, and Kerry saw what turned out to be Aparecida. I remembered being struck by the fact that I had felt only one seamless energy and not two distinct beings. I was being shown something different this time. I was being shown a formless version of the archetypal feminine. The dark void was the dark womb from which all the visible forms of concrete material reality come into existence for a time and later return and are reabsorbed. I now saw the white void as the animating energy of spirit hidden in the forms of the world we see. What I saw was simply a more fundamental version of what Our Lady Aparecida and St. Rita represented. They were personal embodiments of one whole like the Taoist symbol of yin (black) and yang (white).

While I felt an excitement in being greeted by St. Rita and Aparecida before my first trip to Brazil, I felt that the formlessness of the black and white voids gave rise to an expansive, all-embracing awareness. Lying there in the crystal bath, I felt absorbed and contained by velvety darkness. My whole being was enveloped by a deep and all-encompassing peaceful feeling. With the white void, I felt an expansiveness and lightness of being. Rather than a completely restful feeling I felt with the darkness, I experienced an expansive energy that left my body with a slight tingling.

The Void

Once again, the visions of the void were addressing my still being out of balance as a typical mind-dominated male. Space and silence are two aspects of the same thing. I later learned from Eckhart Tolle's *The Power of Now* to think of them as an "externalization" of inner space and inner silence which is stillness, the infinitely creative womb of all existence. I agreed with Eckhart Tolle's observation that most humans are completely "unconscious" of this dimension because I, too, had been out of touch with the stillness within me. When I returned home from Brazil, I began to redress this imbalance by performing a daily practice of taking a few moments here and there to focus on the silence from which sounds arise and fade away. For example, right now, I begin breathing in slowly and deeply, and I hear the sound of an ambulance siren arise and fade back into the silence. I now hear the sound of the ticking of the clock on the mantel and the sound of the heater starting up. Both sounds arise and fade back into the background silence.

Now, I broaden my focus to the space from which all the physical forms I now see appear, and I know they will eventually disappear with the passage of time: the chair I'm sitting in, my computer, the desk, carpet, lamps and so forth. I feel a deep peace as I simply focus on the emptiness of silence and space. I just keep breathing in slowly and deeply while feeling the emptiness of silence and space containing all I hear and see. This includes the people I see walking by in the parking lot and I see cars pull in and leave. I notice the blue sky and white puffy clouds. I also see the Rockford ridge covered by trees rimming the river below.

Again, I find myself thinking of another of Shabkar's poems. It emphasizes the clarity of the consciousness that contains all that we see and hear. He also reminds me that I can access this natural state by being fully alert and awake.

> Once torpor, stupor, and sleepiness
> Have been swept away,
> The natural state of the mind will appear:
> Clear, empty, naked,
> Immaculate like the sky of autumn.

I love how Shabkar reminds us that our true nature is "clear, empty, naked, immaculate like the sky of autumn."

I feel grateful for Shabkar's poems: they remind me that our essential nature is that of the mind empty of content. I AM like the immaculate sky of autumn, gazing down upon the varied oranges, reds, and yellows of the changing leaves; above all, I AM not the contents of my mind; I AM the *content-less consciousness* within which all arises and passes away. I AM the clear, empty, naked, and content-less consciousness who is aware of whatever contents arise moment to moment. These contents include not only the physical ones mentioned above but also mental ones (thoughts) such as the memory of the poached eggs I ate for breakfast and the items I can recall on tomorrow's to-do list, and emotional ones such as the sudden twinge of anxiety I now feel over almost forgetting my appointment with my eye doctor scheduled for tomorrow.

Seeing and sensing the emptiness of the void, of silence and space, was becoming a daily practice in my quest to see clearly. Now I was beginning to see clearly that to be truly *content*, that is, to find true *contentment*, I must see and feel how I AM essentially a content-less consciousness. For, in the crystal bath, I had clearly seen and deeply felt the pervasive peace and contentment that comes with a direct experience of what mystics call the void, and scientists, the field. I would later see how accessing this awareness would be the answer to my request that John of God *reveal* and *remove* the *root* cause of my blindness.

Twelve

Reveal & Remove?

MAY 15, 2012

TEARS SLID SLOWLY DOWN MY CHEEKS SECONDS AFTER I felt the energy of the entities working on me. I had heard Casa guide Heather Cumming suggest that we could ask for the root cause of our ailment to be removed. Given my background as a psychologist, I also wanted to have the root cause revealed. A rapid succession of scenes flashed before me like the fleeting shadows cast on the wall of the cave of memory by the flickering of a candle's flame. The scenes appeared too quickly for me to contemplate them. Still, the scenes brought a continuous flow of tears. I was rapidly reexperiencing situations in early childhood; they were ones in which I felt helpless. My body was at ease and relaxed; I felt every muscle in my body surrender to a complete acceptance of my feelings of helplessness. It was as if I were reviewing each scene and silently repeating what I had labeled the mantra of compassion in *A Matter of Love.* "I know in my heart I would have done differently if I could have done differently but I couldn't so I didn't." There it was: the root cause revealed. It was blocked tears over feeling helpless; and the removal of the root cause was simply accepting my helplessness and allowing tears to flow.

Of course, this allowing was made possible by the energetic support supplied by the entities of light spirit doctors and by the experience of my own essential nature as what Eckhart Tolle had described in *The Power of Now* as the "ever-present I AM, consciousness in its pure state prior to form." A week before leaving for Brazil, I had revisited a core trauma while meditating. Only this time, I was experiencing myself as a formless consciousness, hovering high up in the corner of my childhood bedroom; it was the place where the wall meets the ceiling. As pure consciousness, I was looking down at the back of the head of the 8-year-old me who had just witnessed the body-shuddering screams of my father crawling across the floor as he attempted to make his way to the bathroom. He was in excruciating pain from the back injuries he had suffered in WWII. Suddenly, I saw how the thinking that took place in that 8-year-old head had choreographed the course of my life. This little me made a decision that he would never feel helpless in the face of another's pain. No matter what the cost, even if it killed him, and in some ways it did, he vowed to himself, "I will *never* be helpless again." I'm reminded of the final scene of the first half of the film *Gone With The Wind*. I can see Scarlett O'Hara kneeling on the red earth of Tara in the wake of the devastation of the Civil War, raising her dirt-filled hands to the heavens and vowing she and her kin would never be hungry again. She, too, would never feel helpless again.

Looking at the back of the small brown-haired head, I felt what can be best described as *benevolence*. A cartoon image of this consciousness began to take shape as my inner vision shifted to the vantage point from which I gazed upon the back of the head of the little 8-year-old me. I saw a kind of wispy transparent cloud with a huge red-lipped smile painted on its otherwise formless face. Despite how much havoc had been wreaked on my life by the decision of this little me, so flooded with determination to never feel powerless in the presence of another's pain, I felt no ill will, no anger. There was only a benevolent acceptance, compassion, and empathy.

How surprising it was to see the refusal to accept my helplessness as the root cause of my impaired vision. I was being reminded of what I had seen so often in doing psychotherapy. Simply providing an atmosphere of acceptance empowered patients to release and heal their traumas. The same held true for what appeared to be past-life traumas as well. Later that day, I had an eye-opening experience during a crystal bath. I recalled a lifetime as a healer in ancient Egypt. I had been punished for releasing esoteric material to the masses. My dominant feeling was a burning resentment that the priestly caste had thwarted my efforts to provide the masses with the ancient wisdom hidden away on papyrus scrolls for only the privileged few to see. Strangely, I was not the least bit angry about having my eyes burned out with the red hot tip of a spear.

With the support of my own witnessing presence and the unseen support of the entities, I focused on my resentment. In an instant, the scene shifted and I saw myself atop a stone structure, possibly a pyramid. I was aghast as I watched as thousands were drowning while a handful of us as the privileged priestly caste were safe above the tumult of swirling waters below. I hated feeling helplesss to do anything for the mass of people flailing about as they struggled to hold their heads above the waves. It all became clear to my witnessing consciousness. I had been driven to give out esoteric information to the masses in an attempt to undo my guilt over being helplessly unable to save those thousands from drowning. There was simply not enough room for more than a few of us to be safe from a watery death. My resentment quickly vanished as I suddenly saw the absurdity of attempting to undo my unconscious guilt by giving information to the masses that they could not understand, let alone use. Once again, I was being shown the root cause of my blindness was a refusal to accept my helplessness in the face of the pain and suffering of others. And, again, the removal of the root cause lay in simply accepting that I would have done differently if I could have done differently but I couldn't so I didn't.

On this particular trip to Brazil, I was made even more aware of the presence of unseen support. I was reminded of the biblical passage in the book of Hebrews regarding "so great a cloud of witnesses" cheering us on while helping us "lay aside our weight and sin as we run with perseverance the race that is set before us."

These unseen spirit doctors, these entities of light, were looking on, ready to help us heal.

This idea of unseen support was brought home to me when I returned home and found out that I had missed the last few minutes of the finale of *Desperate Housewives,* a television series I had watched over the last few years. I had enjoyed it for the philosophical musings of the weekly narrator. I had watched the series finale before I left for Brazil but did not realize there was a short segment after the one which I thought contained the final scene of the series. One of the main characters, Susan, was pulling out of her driveway and the contemplative voice of the narrator spoke saying:

> As Susan pulled out of the driveway, she had a feeling that she was being watched, and she was. The ghosts of people who had been a part of Wisteria Lane [the street where the series was set] were gazing upon her as she passed. [The ghosts were lined up along the side of the street. Mike, Susan's beloved husband, was first in what appeared to be a fairly long line.] They watched her as they watch everyone, always hoping the living would put aside rage and sorrow, bitterness and regret. These ghosts watch, wanting people to remember that even the most desperate life is oh so wonderful.

I was stunned by this scene because the ghosts were all dressed in white just like all of us on the days we are to go before John of God. While they looked like us, they were in a role similar to that of the entities of light spirit doctors. I felt that the narrator's comments regarding the ghosts described the concern and caring that the entities had for each and every one of us seeking healing at the Casa: "They [the entities] watch everyone . . . always hoping that the living would put aside rage and sorrow, bitterness and regret. These ghost [entities] watch, wanting people to remember that even the most desperate life is oh so wonderful."

In the segment preceding this final one, we, the viewing audience, hear Johnny Matthis singing the words, "Oh so wonderful." This preceding segment presents the cycle of life. With a 45 record playing on an old phonograph, we hear Johnny Matthis crooning,

"It's wonderful, wonderful, oh so wonderful . . ." while we then watch a juxtaposition of scenes: a wedding, a baby being born, and an elderly woman dying.

    This sequence was no accident. It was a perfect way to punctuate my trip with a reminder of the ever present unseen support. On my next trip, five months later, I would receive an even more dramatic demonstration of unseen allies, offering their guidance and support.

Thirteen

The Octagon Room?

OCTOBER 28, 2012

I WAS AWAKENED IN THE MIDDLE OF THE NIGHT BY A sudden surge of energy entering my body. In my mind's eye, I saw vectors of energy lancing my heart and solar plexus. These vectors appeared as four-inch wide laser beams of golden-white light; they were being shot into me from each of the 8 floor-to-ceiling panes of glass, comprising what was called the octagon room. It was as if I were being electrocuted but it was exhilarating and uplifting, not painful. My mind struggled to grasp what was happening. I had a hazy inner vision of 8 divine feminine figures standing in front of each section of the 8-sided glass room. Set well above the ravine below, the octagon room had a view of the distant ridge over which the sun rose, often lighting up the mist in the ravine. Sometimes the mist looked like the white webbing of a cocoon in which the caterpillar enters and emerges a butterfly. How appropriate! The room was said to create a transformative effect on those who stayed there. Who was there surrounding me? A dream I had just had provided the first clue.

In the dream, there was a group of men dressed in shorts and T-shirts, wearing baseball caps and sneakers. It was a group of stereotypical men's men ready to attend a local sporting event. One stops in his tracks, and says, "Did anyone remember to get Sophie?" (Sophie is a doctoral student in clinical psychology for whom I have been a mentor.) He goes back into the house and brings out Sophie. She is dressed in a white toga-like dress. The pure white of the dress contrasted with her long black hair, pinned up in buns on each side of her head, covering her ears. *Yes*, I thought, *the dream had foretold the identity of the first divine feminine figure, shooting energy into me.* The Greco-Roman style of Sophie's white dress foreshadowed the attire of my first visitor, while the pure white color of Sophie's dress was the color to be worn by all of the divine feminine visitors yet to come.

My first visitor was the goddess Sophia. She was so classically beautiful with her silky shoulder-length black hair and yet her stance before me was so majestic and powerful. How perfect! For, in looking back, hadn't I seen my life since my senior year in college as a search for wisdom? And, wasn't she the one heralded to head the pantheon of divine feminine figures described in this new era of human history (see the section in the prologue that mentions the DVD *Anchored in the Heart*). With this thought of Sophia, I decided to shut off my mind and just surrender to my body awareness of the tremendously powerful energy I was receiving.

The next clue as to the identity of the elegant figure standing next to Sophia came a few hours later, just before dawn. There, in the softly lit predawn sky, hovering over the ridge, I saw what appeared to be a solitary star. It was Venus. I was in the Southern Hemisphere so it made sense to see Venus showing up as the Morning Star in an October sky. Here was the second divine feminine figure who had energized my heart: Venus, the Roman goddess of love. She was radiant as the midday sun in her beauty. Her long golden hair had tints of the hue of a pale pink rose, what some might call strawberry blonde. To me, it was so apt for the color pink is often associated with love. As the days passed, the identities of the others came to me as well as the gifts with which they had infused me.

The rest were revealed to me in the order that they had appeared around the outer perimeter of the octagonally-shaped room. Moving clockwise around the room, the Asian Goddess Quan Yin appeared a few feet from Venus. Instead of her hair being pinned up as I had seen in the crystal-bath vision I'd had of her in 2010, her hair was long and back off of her shoulders; it was as if a gentle breeze were blowing, giving her stunning beauty an etheric quality. She infused me with her gift of ascension power. What did the words ascension power mean? This is what came to me as I contemplated the concept. I recalled the words of Joshua Stone in his book *The Complete Ascension Manual.*

> The consciousness of ascension is that of total joy, total unconditional love, and the complete recognition and realization that you are God and everyone else you meet is God walking on Earth . . . Ascension is the feeling of oneness at all times with God . . .

Shiva was next but not as the male deity worshipped in India today. Instead, Shiva appeared to me as a goddess just as she had during my Reiki class in 1995. She was as heart-stoppingly beautiful as I remembered. Her long black hair, glistening like obsidian, reminded me of a cascading series of small waterfalls flowing over her shoulders. She was wearing a white sari. Shiva infused me with her gift of discernment, symbolized by a ruby-, emerald-, and sapphire-studded golden-handled knife with a silver blade. She had presented this precious symbol to me in the vision I had of her during that Reiki class I attended seventeen years earlier.

The Buddhist goddess, White Tara, appeared next. She had on a head piece that completely covered her head with only her soft white face showing, her countenance so serene and tranquil. Her head piece had a weave and texture, reminding me of chain mail, except it was white and had a kind of widow's peak outlining her forehead. Instead of a classical toga-like dress, she was wearing a white robe, infusing me with the capacity of ever-present and omnipresent compassion. The story of how she first came to me can be found in *A Matter of Love.*

St. Rita, John of God's personal patron saint, was next. She was wearing her white habit and robe and her face was covered with the white veil seen in the photo on the wall of the main hall of the Casa. She infused me with her gift of divine mediumship. I took this to mean helping me be a clear and powerful lens through which the healing energy of the light of divine love shines. In other words, St. Rita was simply infusing me with the power to become a more powerful Reiki healer.

The Brazilian Black Madonna, Our Lady Aparecida, was next. In contrast to how she is usually shown, she was wearing a large white dress that wrapped around her in loose folds so that she was completely covered with only her joyously smiling face showing. She infused me with her gift of connectedness to the heart of the Earth and all creation. Aparecida was helping me see and feel this planet we inhabit to be a living, breathing being: her forests were her lungs, and her rivers, her blood vessels.

Completing the circle was the Egyptian goddess Isis. She had on the kind of classically-styled white dress worn by Sophia, Venus, Quan Yin, and Shiva. Her head was covered with a golden Egyptian head piece that had an asp emerging just above and between her beautiful dark, almost ebony eyes, framed by black, slightly arching brows set in a face with peerlessly perfect features. The asp in the center of her head piece was a symbol of her gift to me. She had infused me with her gift of spiritual vision, often referred to as Horus vision. (Horus is the son of Isis and his symbol is the hawk, a soaring symbol for the transcendent aspect of spiritual vision.) While Aparecida helped me *feel* my body connected to all of the visible world of matter, Isis was enabling me to *feel* my connection with the unseen world of spirit. Along with the spirit doctors, the entities of light of the Casa de Dom Inacio, Isis was helping me connect more deeply with the unseen energy (Reiki) that animates my physical form.

This dramatic visitation was preceded by my finding a small object glowing in the dark immediately after I flipped off the lights and started to pull back my bed covers. I leaned forward and picked up the glowing object. It was a plastic six-pointed star that I later realized had fallen from the base of the rounded area of the white ceiling above my bed. This area contained the tiny inset halogen lights which looked like stars, and when turned off, the after glow gave me the feeling I was in a planetarium, gazing up at the stars. The six-pointed star is often referred to as the Star of

David. The star is comprised of two triangles. With the triangle on top pointing toward the sky and the one on the bottom pointing toward the ground, their intersection is said to symbolize the union of Heaven and Earth, spirit and matter, soul and body, the higher self and lower self, the divine masculine and the divine feminine. Attaining an inner union or sacred inner marriage of these opposites had emerged into my awareness as a key part of my healing; and, from what I had heard from my guide Chris, it was an essential element in all the healing taking place at the Casa. I climbed into bed and decided I would meditate with the little glowing star so laden with meaning. I began meditating with it on my heart and, after a few minutes, I placed it on my forehead, slightly above and between my eyes, and drifted off to sleep. As I mentioned in an earlier chapter, this is the area associated with spiritual vision, also referred to as the sixth chakra or third eye.

As amazing as this visitation was, I realized that it was not out of nowhere that it happened. But it was not only my meditation that seemed to summon the support of the divine feminine. It was directly related to the other request I presented to John of God. In addition to asking for my sight to be restored, I had asked, "Please expand and deepen my spiritual vision." As I write these words, I find myself thinking how important it is to keep remembering to do as Christ said, "Ask, and it will be given you; seek, and you will find; knock, and it will be opened to you" (Matthew 7:7-8). I had and it was. But now, the trick is to keep remembering to *remind* myself to keep asking and to be sure to pay attention to what follows because what follows is always related to what I ask for, even if, at first glance, it does not appear to be connected in any obvious way.

What was begun that night in this room with its 360 degree view was a microcosm of what was happening all over the planet. My mind-dominated male consciousness, focused on *doing*, was being infused with gifts of the feminine with their emphasis on *being*. As I mentioned earlier, Carl Jung had predicted the reemergence of the feminine to counter balance the overly male emphasis of the last two thousand years.

The presence of these divine feminine figures infusing my body with their gifts was a foreshadowing of how the entities of light, the spirit doctors, would work with me during and following my next two invisible spiritual surgeries. They would work within my thoughts, infusing my mind with a constant flow of passages from my own books. They were reminding me, or, I should say, re-*mind*-ing me, of tools and techniques I had developed for shifting anger, fear, sadness, and depression back to love. And, why not? After all, the longstanding message, dating back to the dawn of the new millennium, was that I would regain my sight when I could see with "total love and no fear." They were simply reminding me of just how that could be accomplished. John Donne's words soared into my mind, "A man's reach should exceed his grasp, or what's a heaven for?"

It was now November 1st, All Saints Day. How fitting! I could now call it *All Entities of Light Day*, some of whom were saints. My invisible surgery took place on Wednesday, October 31st, the afternoon of Halloween. Moments before I entered the Casa for surgery, I was beginning to feel some doubt as to whether I'd ever get my sight back. Right then, I heard a woman in the Main Hall enthusiastically announce, "A man who has been blind from birth just received his sight and is now seeing for the first time." I thought of the passage from the Bible when Jesus healed a man, blind from birth, who called out, "One thing I do know, I was blind but now I see" (John 9:25). Once again, as soon as a little doubt crept in as to whether I'd ever get my sight back, it was immediately addressed as it had been on that airport ride in 2010. As you may recall, it was then that I'd hear how a legally-blind physician cried tears of joy when he got his sight back. He had exclaimed, "I can see! I can see!"

As I think about it now, it seems significant that the first segment of my twenty-four hour, post-surgery rest period took place on October 31st, Halloween, All Hallow's Eve. I had found, and heard from others, how the rest period can be a dark-night of the soul. In this rest period, I'd see how the spirit doctor entities of light strive to help us confront and release our fears, or, you could say, in the spirit of Halloween, unmask and release our personal demons.

I was halfway into my rest period when I noticed something different from past post-surgery rest periods. I was not feeling those occasional flutters of energy, indicating that the entities were continuing to work on me. Then, I had a sudden flash of insight. All those passages from my own books that were popping into my thoughts were not coming from me but from the spirit doctors. They were using their energy to enter my mind and direct my thoughts. Like invisible mental sculptors, they were literally fashioning and shaping my mind by *re-mind-ing* me of how I could use my own writings and favorite passages from other writings, such as those found in *A Course in Miracles,* to practice seeing as God sees with total love and no fear as Christ saw his persecutors from the cross.

I found myself thinking of how God is love and, as I had written in *8 Steps to Love*, that "love was nothing less than God, the ultimate power operating in the universe." The entities reminded me that the first section of *8 Steps to Love* was entitled "Love Is Who You Are."

When I awoke in the middle of the night, the spirit doctors gave me an opportunity to practice shifting back to love. A fly was buzzing around the room. I was instantly annoyed and got up to grab something to swat it. But then I stopped myself, telepathically speaking my mind to the mind of the fly. "I AM love and I know that you, too, are love. I will not harm you. I will respect your physical boundaries, and I expect you to respect mine." The annoying buzzing stopped. Still, I opened the screen door on the balcony for a minute or so. I couldn't tell if the fly flew out or not. I wondered if he were simply something the entities manifested for my practice. I closed the screen door to the balcony and decided it would be a good idea to make my way to the bathroom. I opened the glass door to my room and walked across the outdoor patio to the small building that housed the bathroom. As I entered the bathroom, I flipped on the light. Immediately, an instinctual fear of creepy crawly creatures, spiders, snakes, and so forth shot through me. My eyes had quickly narrowed their focus, telescoping in on a slimy brown-speckled creature resembling a walking toad stool about three inches in diameter. It was positioned on the wall right next to the toilet. *Oh*, I thought, *here's another opportunity to practice.* I sent the same message as I did to the fly, and I had once again shifted from a focus colored by fear to seeing through the clear and powerful lens of love. I was seeing beyond the veil of the multiplicity of life forms and the idea that I am separate from them. I could now see how all these separate physical forms were connected; they were infused with the energy of love and pure consciousness. And, from our essence as the energy of love and consciousness, I could now see how every one of us could communicate silently with all that is.

Drifting back to sleep, the spirit doctor entities of light turned my attention to an affirmation I had written in *8 Steps to Love,* addressing God as the Divine Beloved. The words had come to me following a mystical experience I had had just before sunrise on the Spring Equinox of 1998. (For a detailed description of that seminal moment in my spiritual life, see *A Matter of Love* and/or *The Space Between Stars*.) I was in the inner sanctuary of the Temple of the Moon in Tikal, Guatemala, where I had been studying with the Maya. The entities seemed to be presenting it as a prayerful lullaby *reminding* me: "*I AM never separated from the expansive energy and peaceful power of the light of Your pure everlasting love. For in the core of my being, my innermost heart, I AM the expansive energy and peaceful power of the light of Your pure everlasting love.*"

Fourteen

Surrendered Seeing?

MARCH 17, 2013

SOMETHING IS HAPPENING? BUT WHAT IS IT? Surrendered seeing—that's it! I am now seeing through being, not doing. I no longer do the seeing. God or love or being does. I am being seen through, and I am not limited by my body's eyes. For one thing, I had had many different sets of eyes in different bodies. I was now seeing that I was not those bodies, and my true self was the invisible awareness that was seeing through the eyes of the crusader, the Andromedan, the Native American brave, and the cavalry soldier who lay wounded in the ditch.

Hadn't I seen a fundamental truth in that old church yard at an early age? The words etched into the gravestone read:

All that's bright must fade
All that's fair decay
All that we loved was made
To bloom and pass away

I saw this testimony to the impermanence of this world we live in the next day after what was perhaps the best I ever played in any basketball game at any level: high school, college or professionally. It was the college game I described in *The Space Between Stars*. I was in the zone. I aligned myself to the flow of the game. And, these stark words on the gravestone aligned me to the ebb and flow of human life. They did not dampen my celebratory mood but gave me an unexpected peace.

These sobering words followed me through life and influenced my work as a psychologist. Hadn't I been shown in doing psychotherapy—with so many people in the midst of suffering—that suffering simply involved not accepting what is, even arguing with what is? After all, I'd heard so many patients complain: "It shouldn't be that way. My wife should be more understanding. My husband should be more considerate." And, hadn't I worked hard to help patients realize it is best to accept the truth of what is and make the most of it?

In helping others and in reflecting on my own life, I learned to find deep peace by accepting the words on that gravestone. Now, through my trips to Abadiania, I was realizing I had been in many forms and that forms arise and pass away. I now felt that there was a peace that passed understanding. I was waking up out of identification with content, with form. I was not any one of those bodies I had seen in the crystal bath visions. I was something else. I was the one who was angry and tearful that we keep coming back and each time, after we are born, we face the same formula, repeat the same mantra: *live, love, lose, die; live, love, lose, die.* But I was discovering a great peace as I not only accepted but *felt* in the very cells of my current body the truth of the fact that all that's bright must fade, all that's fair decay, all that we loved was made to bloom and pass away. Somehow I was surrendering to this given fact of human existence, and I felt peace and I felt a feeling of being fully alive as though I had awakened from a dream that was a dance of matter, of form, appearing for a time and disappearing. Shabkar's poem described it so well. I had been that "setting sun resplendent with light, passing beyond the western summit to reappear again soon above the mountains of the East."

Great joy seemed to come from the idea of surrendering as a knight on one knee and accepting my limits. And, as my Jungian analyst, David Hart, had taught me back in 1973, it is at the moment of surrender that something beyond my little body- or form-based self experiences something beyond its limits, something limitless. David Hart had spoken of the hero in the fairy tale finding the solution to his quest to rescue the princess held captive in the castle. Now, after my vision of myself as a knight, a crusader, I knew why I had always pictured a kneeling knight.

I was learning to surrender, to say yes, to what was appearing to me in each moment. For example, I was waiting for a loved one who had broken her leg and was scheduled to arrive at New York Hospital in New York City. I felt peace as hours passed, and I remained alert but not anxious as I waited to greet her. I wanted her to be greeted by a familiar friendly face in such a time of pain and fear. I sat back and waited, aligning myself with the background of silence, and the implied emptiness of the space in which all of the hustle and bustle of the hospital's admission area was arising and passing away: sirens blaring, garbage trucks banging dumpsters, one ambulance after another arriving and one patient after another being wheeled in on stretchers. I was experiencing an awareness that was beyond and embraced the opposites, good and bad, pain and relief of pain, in the midst of all that clamor, all that harried rushing. I was in the vastness Shabkar wrote of in his poems. I was alert and lucid, letting my gaze encompass the infinity of the sky. I was the sky, empty and luminous, beyond all attachments, watching the setting sun of forms of life, racing about in that endless moment. There was no little me engaged in self talk about what I liked and didn't like.

I now had a sense of the peace of the emptiness left by forms of life dissolving. Loss of a person leaves a space as happened when my little auntie recently died, leaving her special spot on the couch empty. But then she had come to me to teach me on the day of her funeral. I was awakened by the sound of her walker. I got a picture in my mind of her moving down the hall to the bathroom. The little me, the embodied soul was angry and sad that all is impermanent. But was it? Wasn't it permanently impermanent? Wasn't there an implied backdrop to all this arising and passing away? Moments after seeing my little auntie motoring along, I heard a sound by the television set. She was politely letting me know she was on her way to me. Then, I felt as though a magic carpet of energy slid under me and lifted me in undulating waves as I lay on my bed. Clearly, she was appearing in a different form.

And then, after I posted my blog entry entitled, "My Little Auntie: A Model for Us All," another message came through. I clicked on the icon to publish my blog entry and then a blog from three months earlier popped up on the screen. A phrase in the middle of my blog was highlighted: "Consciousness is awakening from its disguise as form." My little auntie's sense of humor was coming through and she was winking at me, using the language I was using to describe my vision quest. I was learning to surrender to, even embrace, the emptiness that the form, whether a person or a prized possession, leaves behind. I was now feeling joy in the emptiness, the space left, instead of being seized by sadness. I could see how loss can lead to the peace that passes understanding.

I had had one loss after another so that my life was like a large piece of Swiss Cheese. Looking back, I could see how I was becoming acquainted with emptiness: I left my private practice, I gave up the two houses I owned, got rid of my car, and reduced all my belongings to what would fit in a duffle bag. But in all the holes, I had been gradually waking up out of identification with things, possessions, accomplishments, to realize I was none of that. But now with my trips to Brazil, I was beginning to see what so many sages had said: this was a dream, even if it seemed to be a very real dream, and the way out of it was accepting the dream and all its images and doing what I could to make it a "happy dream" as *A Course in Miracles* advises. I was waking up out of identification with all kinds of form: my various bodies, the various forms my life had taken. I had been a psychologist, a healer, a writer, and in visions I had lifetimes in different bodies.

I could now see that suffering originates in not accepting or forgiving what is in our lives whether in our relationships or our life circumstances. Rather than complain, we need to first accept the truth of the gap between what is and what we would love to have happen. Then we can seek to close the gap by focusing on and bringing about what we would love instead of what is. When people would greet my little auntie and ask her how she was doing, she would inevitably say, "No complaints. It wouldn't do any good anyway." She was so right. But more than no complaints, surrendered seeing involved what I heard after boarding the plane bound for home.

Climbing into my seat, I heard the soulful-sounding voice of a black woman singing, "I'm in love with everything I see. . . ." The pilot's voice cut in over the intercom, interrupting the song; no more of the song was heard. The engines roared, and we started down the runway, gaining speed for take-off. Perfect! No more words were needed. This was what surrendered seeing was all about. This line from the song not only incorporated my affirmation to see as God sees with total love and no fear, it went way beyond it.

While I write these words, I see large pristine snowflakes falling outside my office window. I'm in love with each flake. I even imagine being in love with the pure white snow becoming blackened, something I would have not thought possible before. Yes, in anticipation of the snow stopping, trucks plowing, and picturing dirt and grime from the road robbing the snow of its purity, I find myself saying yes to the dirty snow. Yes, I'm in love with the dirty snow. Of course, I realize that the contrast makes the pure white snow even more precious as does getting hot and sweaty from jogging makes a cool drink a true treasure. But that's not the point. It's all part of what I've heard Eckhart Tolle refer to as "the good that has no opposite." I suppose this is what the Celts meant in their reference to God. The celtic word God means good. Seeing through God's eyes means seeing it as all good, even the good, the bad, and the ugly. I was imagining how I could be in love with and not repulsed by the large hairy-legged spider I'd seen in Brazil. Grotesque forms or inherently beautiful forms, I was seeing how I could be in love with it all arising and passing away within the spaciousness of my awareness.

Yes, I was finally beginning to see as God sees even if my vision was not 20/20. And yet, perhaps, like the two women who see without the use of their optic nerves, I, too, will see this material world more clearly through the eyes of spirit, my true self. I was prepared for my upcoming trip to go before John of God once again.

Fifteen

Turning It Over?

MAY 30, 2013

"He's asking if you want him to operate on your eyes now with a visible surgery or wait until tomorrow to have an invisible surgery." The translator's words so stunned me. I was that proverbial deer paralyzed by a car's headlights. Should I go under the knife or wait? Competing thoughts, the pros and cons, crowded my mind with the thundering force of that thick cluster of cars, all vying for the lead, at the opening of a race on a Nascar speedway. The cons took the lead at first, but eventually the pros overtook them, and won out in the end.

    I had had many surgeries in both eyes, major, under-the-scalpel surgery, including surgery for a retinal detachment in my right eye many years earlier. And, to have John of God do a visible surgery was risky. I knew from my ophthalmologist that for someone with glaucoma, the least little impact on the eye could cause a detached retina. But that was under ordinary conditions and John of God's surgeries were anything but ordinary. No anesthetic was used. He used an ordinary kitchen knife that was never sterilized. In over fifty years, no one has ever suffered an infection and, if there is any pain, it has usually been described as minimal. These alone were miracles in addition to six or more men and women who had had their sight restored and the two I had heard received sight after being blind from birth. I then thought of Christ's healing of the sight of the man born blind (John 9:`25). And, today, May 30th, was celebrated as *Corpus Christi* in Brazil, and throughout the world by all Catholics, Anglicans, and Episcopalians, the tradition within which I was raised. Here, on the day celebrating the body and blood of Christ, the Eucharist, Holy Communion, I was being offered a visible, on-my-body, surgery. This meant my body would be operated on directly by John of God. I knew this was significant but just how I did not have time to consider. I needed to make a decision. I did know from my previous trips that I did not meet the age criteria necessary for a visible surgery. I was outside the age range of 18 to 52.

Clearly, this was some kind of special dispensation. And why not? *Hadn't I turned the trip over to the Holy Spirit?* Moreover, moments before my standing before John of God, I'd spoken a silent prayer, reaffirming my intention to take whatever John of God said or did in response to my requests as a sign from the Holy Spirit. Then, one final thought drove my decision over the finish line: *Hadn't I been prepared by Rod, my traveling companion on my first trip to see John of God in 2009?* Just four days before departing on this trip, Rod and I were having lunch, when he showed me a book he'd recently come across about John of God. The title contained the very instrument he would use to perform a visible surgery on me: *The Brazilian Healer with a Kitchen Knife*. Of all the books I'd ever heard about him, *none* had featured the knife.

"Visible surgery," I answered, addressing the translator. He had asked me to decide which surgery I wanted: visible now or invisible tomorrow? I was flying on the wings of faith as the translator and another man immediately spun me around and seated me in a wheelchair. Lyrics from an old country song floated into my mind, "On the wings of a snow white dove . . ." I asked myself, *Was that the voice of Johnny Cash or Ferlin Husky, describing the dove, an age-old symbol of the Holy Spirit?* Either way, I knew the Holy Spirit was using the heartfelt words and voice of an old-time country crooner to comfort and reassure me. I felt as if I were being carried forth by the Comforter, another name of the Holy Spirit, into John of God's capable hands as well as into the invisible hands of the spirit doctors entities of light. And yet, the strange thing was that I could actually feel those unseen hands. Being touched by them felt just as solid and real as the touch of a physical hand.

I thought back to an afternoon session when I was sitting in current (meditating) in the area of the Casa close to where John of God sits; it was on my previous trip in October, 2012, seven months earlier. I had felt a hand firmly grip my right shoulder but saw no one. Then I heard a voice in my mind, and, with my mind's eye, saw Dom Inacio. He was saying, "You are my son." That didn't mean that I was somehow special. After all, it was in *The Space Between Stars*, that I'd written, "With faith we become sons and daughters of the Most High." Certainly, all of us seeking healing had demonstrated faith by simply coming to the Casa.

Curiously, it seems that Dom Inacio had been with me from the very start of that trip to the Casa in October. When I had boarded the plane in Philadelphia to begin my trip, I had heard the pilot speaking over the intercom, "This is your pilot, Inacio." I couldn't believe my ears. I turned to the woman seated next to me and asked her what she heard the pilot say his name was. I made sure I did not state what I'd heard him say. I wanted to be careful not to ask a leading question because I wanted to be certain that I wasn't imagining what I'd heard. I discovered I'd heard correctly. She verified that he had indeed identified himself as "Inacio." Now the feeling of invisible hands holding me in place as John of God prepared to operate was not startling to me.

With John of God cradling my head with his left hand and the kitchen knife in his right, I was surprised to feel a rush of cool water flowing into my eye. *Why this is exactly like having surgery with my ophthalmologist,* I thought excitedly. *My eye is being hydrated. I was looking up through a soothing pool of cool water.* It was not until I saw the DVD of my surgery after I'd returned home that I could see no one was pouring water into my eye. I immediately recalled a sermon I once heard in which a priest had described water, wind, and fire as some of the ways that the presence of the Holy Spirit was made known to us during trying times. Here was yet another sign that the world of spirit was supporting and guiding my surgery; and my decision to surrender my surgery into the Hands of the Holy Spirit had indeed summoned the support of the Comforter.

As soon as John of God had finished operating, I was wheeled back to the recovery room where I was greeted by two of the women who assist people after their visible surgeries. One helped me onto a bed while the other bandaged my eye with a patch of gauze and tape. She then filled a small rubber surgical glove with ice and placed it over the gauze covering my eye. I rested for approximately forty-five minutes, and was driven back to my room to sleep as much as possible over the next twenty-four hours. My pain was minimal and the discomfort I'd felt the first few hours after the operation was completely gone by morning. My eye felt normal and I slept until my twenty-four hour rest period ended on Friday night at 6:30.

On Saturday morning, June 1st, the first full day after my surgery and the required rest period, I awoke in the Octagon Room to see the sun starting its ascent above the ridge. I had decided to stay in this special room so that I could see those enchanting sunrises I had witnessed on my previous trip. I walked out onto the balcony and found a beautiful blue and white flower in the center of one of the two white wrought iron chairs on the balcony of the Octagon Room. The colors were those of Mother Mary, and, in Her honor, these were the colors painted on the outside of all the buildings on the sacred grounds of the Casa. What happened next was the beginning of a series of signs that the Holy Spirit was communicating to me.

I turned on my cell phone (Apple iPhone 5) but not for calls. I'd downloaded music as well as a number of spiritual books and talks that I could listen to since I had traveled alone on this trip. I did not have a traveling companion to read to me as I'd had on other trips. Since I did not want to incur roaming charges on my cell phone, I did not want to use the audio feature (Siri) to select specific books, talks or music. Somehow the shuffle feature was on and books, talks, and music were selected at random, or, so it seemed. Whatever was selected was always relevant to the three requests I'd made when going before John of God. They were part of my healing. The first one I heard following my finding the flower was the Buddhist monk and spiritual teacher, Thich Naht Hahn, teaching mindfulness meditation. The recording began well into his talk. I knew this because I'd listened to the whole CD months before. "Breathing in, I see myself as a flower. Breathing out, I feel fresh." He went on to say that human beings are flowers, especially as innocent children. He described how our eyes and lips are flowers so that when we smile at others, we are presenting flowers to them. Talk about seeing with total love and no fear, the mantra for the healing of my vision, this teaching of Thich Naht Hahn fit perfectly. I won't go into all of the amazing synchronicities that followed from the shuffle feature on my phone because I would have to sacrifice the brevity of focus I've been trying to achieve in this book. I will, however, select a few examples to illustrate the presence of the Holy Spirit, guiding the healing process.

This is truly the dawn of a new day in more ways than one, I thought. The sun was now in full view over the ridge which was significant to me since it had been cloudy for the last few days, mirroring my glaucoma-damaged vision. I thought, *Perhaps this is an omen that my sight will be restored.* I was smiling to myself as I gazed upon the beautiful blue-and-white flower. It seemed that unseen hands had picked and placed it there before me. I'd made the same two requests I'd always made on all my trips to the Casa. "Please restore my eyesight," and, "Please expand and deepen my spiritual sight." It took me a few days, but, after much reflection, I carefully crafted the following request to present to John of God: "Please reveal and remove any obstacles to my receiving restored vision." The visible operation as well as all the synchronicities that followed appeared to be an answer to that request. . . .

On my trip in May, 2012, I had asked for the root cause to be revealed and removed; but now I suspected something within me, possibly from early childhood, was blocking my receiving restored sight. Guilt? Anger? Fear? Self-condemnation?

All of the above had entered my thoughts following a dream I'd had involving the young woman I'd married in 1982 and was divorced from in 1984. *Why had I dreamt of her?* I wondered. Then, feeling annoyed with myself, I wondered, *Why had I found myself getting involved with women whose fathers had in some way, either actually and/or emotionally, abandoned them? Women who, as a result, were struggling financially?* This woman had been the first in a series. But why? Then it struck me. In getting involved with these women, I was attempting to undo guilt I had felt over my father losing his ability to work at his job with the DuPont Company when I was 12-years-old. In *Words Become Flesh* and in *The Space Between Stars*, I traced the origin of my glaucoma to the guilt I'd repressed over my *oedipal* competition with my father for my mother's attention. But now I awoke, realizing there was also a more primal guilt I'd unconsciously sought to undo.

My father had lost everything, all his savings he had put into a business with my Uncle Vinnie when the third partner absconded with all the funds. I came into the world feeling guilty for being born and being a burden. At some deeper level, my soul had recorded my father not wanting me because he could not afford another mouth to feed.

Over the years, I had uncovered the layers of my deeply repressed oedipal guilt and self-condemnation. When I was growing up, I recall my mother using a fork to gently tease apart the thick pile of thinly sliced lunch meats, often boiled ham or bologna. Similarly, over a span of thirty years, I had to use the fork of insight to uncover and separate the layers of my oedipal guilt. The first layer was lifted in a session with an analyst in 1985, three months after my father died. I remember recalling how I hated myself for being small and helpless and unable to relieve my father's physical pain. He often suffered from back injuries sustained in World War II. Ten years later, in 1995, I was in a spiritually-oriented therapy session, and I discovered I had been angry at God for being all-powerful and not taking my father's pain away. Ten years after that, in 2005, I awoke from a dream in which I had cried out to God: "How can You let me see my wishes come true?" My competitive oedipal wish was to bring my father to his knees. So I now realized that I'd felt God had let me see my wishes come true on that traumatic night when I was 8 years old. I saw him on his hands and knees, crawling to the bathroom, screaming in pain, and waving my mother away, refusing her help. And, I was angry at God—I was angry that God left me holding the bag—the bag of guilt.

Each time I lifted yet another layer of guilt, I felt the guilt drop away. This morning was no different. In answer to my question about why I had gotten involved with women with financial difficulties, I could now *see* it was an unconscious and ineffective, albeit costly, effort to undo my guilt. The next selections on my cell phone revealed another way of undoing guilt, one that gets to the core of the problem and is therefore effective.

The first selection came from *The Disappearance of the Universe*. "Use your mind to choose between the body and true spirit, and by doing so forgive the world." *Forgive the world?* I thought. *What did that mean?* The next passage on the same track provided the answer. It was a quotation from *A Course in Miracles* that continued the focus on the contrast of choosing spirit over the body.

> Salvation is undoing. If you choose to see the body, you behold a world of separation, unrelated things, and happenings that make no sense at all. This one appears and disappears in death; that one is doomed to suffering and loss. And no one is exactly as he was an instant previous, nor will he be as he is now an instant hence. Who could have trust where so much change is seen, for who is worthy if he be but dust? Salvation is undoing of all this. For constancy arises in the sight of those whose eyes salvation has released from looking at the cost of keeping guilt, because they chose to let it go instead.

Later that day, I resumed listening to my cell phone's selections. The same quotation regarding salvation came up again, only it was from a different source, a talk given by Gary Renard, whom you may recall, is author of *The Disappearance of the Universe*. The talk was entitled, *Fearless Love*. The title was a beautifully succinct expression of my quest to see with total love and no fear. This repeated passage on what constitutes salvation, undoing guilt, and projected guilt (anger), by seeing with forgiving eyes, held the key to my removing the blocks to my receiving restored sight. It contained a reference to the anger I'd felt regarding how we all *live, love, lose* and *die*. Could I forgive the world? Or, more precisely, could I forgive, that is, accept this pattern of impermanence? Then there was the reference to releasing guilt. But I knew guilt involved more than my own feelings of guilt and being unforgiving toward myself. The answer lay in the releasing, or, letting go, of guilt whether my own or that projected onto, or, you might say, assigned to others. Projected guilt is anger and blame; it amounts to finding fault in others and leads to unforgiveness. But what I'd found was more about guilt and self-condemnation that I'd experienced directly. I forgave myself and my father. I was also forgiving the world for its fleeting impermanence. I was undoing my little ego self's story of this, or any previous lifetime. Instead, I was identifying with my spirit, seeing and feeling myself as love itself. I was experiencing my essence as the silence within which all sound emerges and fades away, and the spacious awareness within which all forms, inner and outer, arise and pass away.

A few hours later, I went to the local café where I overheard a man speaking about *A Course in Miracles*. I approached him, and he invited me to attend a local Course in Miracles study group. At the study group, we did what one group member called "bibliomancy." The woman hosting the group meeting opened the book at random to see what message the Holy Spirit might have for us as a group before we did so for each of us as individuals. The passage she read to us was from chapter 8, section 9: *Healing as Corrected Perception*. It spoke directly to what I'd wondered about the healing of the body: "When the ego tempts you to sickness, do not ask the Holy Spirit to heal the body for this would merely be to accept the ego's belief that the body is the proper aim of healing." *Wow!* I thought. I then told the group, "Just yesterday, I was trying to remember what the Course says about physical healing," Then our hostess continued reading, "Ask, rather, that the Holy Spirit teach you the right perception of the body."

Just what was the right perception of the body, I wondered, appreciating what I was hearing. I felt blessed. I listened closely for passages on healing. Then I heard our hostess read the phrase, "all healing involves replacing fear with love." She then read from the end of the previous section, "Health is the result of relinquishing all attempts to use the body lovelessly." And so, I was being shown that we get sick when we use the body "lovelessly," that is, when we judge and attack others and ourselves. I had locked myself in a prison of self-condemnation and thrown away the key. But the key was now being handed back to me by the Holy Spirit. We undo this fault-finding tendency of our little body-based identity, the ego, by forgiving others and ourselves.

When I randomly opened the book, I was guided to Lesson 42 from the workbook section of the course: "God is my strength. Vision is His gift." All of us in the group were astonished. The Holy Spirit was truly guiding me as I had asked by turning the trip over to the care of the Comforter.

The next morning my cell phone shuffle started playing another track from Gary Renard's talk, *Fearless Love*. I heard him say, referring to *A Course in Miracles*, "The way Jesus puts it in the course, 'The message of the Crucifixion is perfectly clear: teach only love for that is what you are.'" So my surgery being on the day celebrating *Corpus Christi,* the body and blood of Christ, held this message of love. It was what I'd be focusing on for a while; I was working on seeing with total love, no anger and no fear as Christ saw his persecutors from the Cross.

Right after I returned home, I contacted Dr. Elisabeth Webb, a homeopathic and naturopathic doctor, who grew up in Brazil and spoke Brazilian Portuguese. I wanted her to watch the DVD of my surgery so she could translate what John of God had said during my surgery. She began by telling me, "He's asking one of the men watching to hold the light a little closer." She continued, "Now he's saying, 'I remove this forever!' And now, as he looks up, he's saying, 'Is there anything else I need to do?' He seems to be asking for guidance by addressing God or the other spirit doctors." She then said, "He's now asking the two men if they saw the entities scraping the eye? They're indicating that they did see the entities at work. And now, as he grabs the right side of his own neck with his right hand, he's saying, 'I believe the problem comes from here . . .'" The segment showing my surgery ends abruptly and another person's surgery begins. Elisabeth concludes, saying, "But the person recording this cut off the rest of what John of God is saying. I believe he was saying it has something to do with your throat, perhaps something you feel or felt that you repressed and choked back. There may be something you need to express."

What was John of God saying, or, more precisely, what was José Valdivino, saying? Various volunteer staff at the Casa told me that he was the spirit doctor entity of light who was operating through John of God that day. I immediately thought of the passage in the Bible about projection and called Rod to find it for me. He did and it is as follows:

> Why do you see the speck that is in your brother's eye, but do not notice the log that is in your own eye? . . . first take the log out of your own eye, and then you will see clearly to take the speck out of your brother's eye (Matthew 7:3-5).

Was John of God removing the log that I'd projected over many lifetimes? Was he removing the log of unconscious guilt that we all repress, the guilt over believing we separated from God, from love? The log of guilt that leads us to project guilt onto others? The log of guilt and fear we bury within us that drives us to incarnate over and over again? The log of guilt that created this illusory universe that feels so real? Yes. The Holy Spirit had guided me to this passage. The message was the one mentioned earlier. It was given by Christ to St.Thomas: "To return home [to God], forgive your brother for only then do you forgive yourself." Of course, the reverse is true as well. If we forgive ourselves, we are more likely to project forgiveness to others instead of guilt.

An inspiring synchronicity occurred on the final day of this trip to Abadiania, just two hours before I was to leave for the airport to fly home. I happened to meet and talk with Bob, a man whose sight had been restored after a number of trips to see John of God. Right before I left on this trip, I heard about Bob's quest for restored vision. Rod read Bob's story to me. It was featured in the book *The Brazilian Healer with a Kitchen Knife*. Now, Bob was before me and I got to ask him, "Bob, how many spiritual surgeriess did you have before your sight was restored?" Bob answered, "Ten, and the last one was a visible one." I was stunned because that matched my own number of surgeries exactly. I'd had ten also, nine invisible surgeries with the last one I'd just had being a visible one. My trip had been bookended by Bob's successs story.

Perhaps this synchronicity in the number and sequence of surgeries is a sign, an omen, that I'll follow in Bob's footsteps. Still, I feel I've been blessed already; my condition is stable and has been since I started going to the Casa in 2009. Glaucoma generally has a gloomy prognosis. I've been told by the various eye doctors I've seen that it is a progressive disease that leads to total blindness. All Western medicine can do is slow down the progression with various types of surgery and eye drops. So far, since seeing John of God, the progression has been halted, not simply delayed.

As for now, I'm grateful I see well enough to get around in this world of matter, so I don't get hit by a truck when crossing the street. I also feel thankful to and blessed by John of God and the entities for helping me truly experience who I AM: spirit, consciousness, awakening from the dream of matter, form, and the erroneous belief that I, and you as well, are separate from God. I AM, as are you, a finger on the infinite Hand of God, hidden in the glove of physical form, and forever pointing to the truth that we are much more than this finite physical form. We are all transparent eyes of God. Ralph Waldo Emerson said it so beautifully:

> In the woods we return to reason and faith. . . . Standing on bare ground—my head bathed by the blithe air and uplifted into infinite space—all mean egotism vanishes. I become a transparent eyeball. I am nothing. I see all. The currents of the Universal Being circulate through me; I am part or particle of God.

Epilogue

Feel to Heal?

AUGUST 15, 2013

ONE PERSISTENT THEME EMERGED ON MY TRIPS to the Casa—the physical was not important. I did not have to have my optic nerves regenerated as I had first thought. Those two women I'd heard of had perfect sight and non-functioning optic nerves. But then I had just had a visible surgery involving my body and not just on any day but on a very special one. I could now see another reason why it was so significant that my visible, on-the-body, operation occurred on *Corpus Christi*, celebrating the body and blood of Christ. The Holy Spirit had led me back to the body to go beyond my finite physical form. I was to get back to the body as a portal to spirit instead of trying to deny it or trying to leave it in out-of-body experiences.

    The return to the body and especially the life—the very feeling of the aliveness—in the body had begun during and following my October, 2012 trip to the Casa. The eight divine feminine figures had heightened my awareness of my body, providing me with a tremendous infusion of energy into my body. Then, after I returned home, I felt the entities come to me during my revision ritual. They infused my hands and feet as well as my pelvic area with energy. I experienced a feeling of potency radiating from these three distinct areas of my body. The first chakra with its focus on survival, and second chakra with its focus on sex and cre-activity are both in the pelvic area. *Hands are for doing and making, feet are for grounding, and the pelvic area is for procreation and creation,* I reasoned.

What did all this mean? What would I do from here? I would continue my daily practice of aspiring to see as God sees. But how? What was my next step? When I'd asked in the Good-Bye Line at the end of my trip in 2009, I sat quietly in the surgery room. I immediately felt a flood of feeling in my hands, a feeling of aliveness. What were the entities saying with this infusion of feeling, of energy? Instantly, I thought, *What are the entities telling me? The power is in my hands? If so, what does that mean? My healing* is *in my hands. It's up to me.* But not just by placing my own hands on my eyes. It was more about a shift in consciousness, a shift in my sense of myself. Eckhart Tolle's words from his talk, *Gateways to the Now*, came to me. He'd said something about there being an old saying that "God is closer than your hands and feet." Then he went on to say that as close as hands and feet are, it's the very "aliveness" in your hands and feet that is even closer. What he then said really summed up what I was experiencing, "It is not a sacrilege to say that the nearest God is to you is in your body. God is the very life that you are."

I was not separate from the life hidden in all forms of life. To heal I was to be sure to consciously *feel* the aliveness throughout my body and in my eyes. I was to shift away from thinking and focus on *feeling* to facilitate my healing.

Could it be that simple? Yes. To be one with God and not separate was the key. Or, rather to realize none of us is separate from the life in us, from God, from love. I find myself remembering the words of Dr. Bruce Goldberg from the National Hypnotherapy Convention I'd attended in 1994, "See it. Feel it. And it becomes reality." For years, I'd emphasize that we need to fill the gap between what is and what we would love to have happen by feeling good first, that is, before the desired outcome is attained and not after. Therefore, I have and will continue to set aside some time each day, *seeing* myself *seeing* more clearly through soft forgiving eyes that look upon the world with total love and no fear.

Epilogue

And all the while, I will be *feeling* the excitement that this visualization generates in my body. I will be sure to feel good first as I *feel* to heal.

* * *

"I AM MORE THAN MY PHYSICAL BODY," I HEARD ROBERT Monroe say. It was now just two months since my return from my last trip to Brazil, and I was listening to one of his Hemi-Sync CDs. As so often happens, I was led to the next step on my spiritual path and healing journey when I was inspired by a friend to attend a series of workshops at the Monroe Institute in Virginia. The process of synchronizing the left and right hemispheres of the brain, developed by Monroe, reminded me of the healing emphasis at the Casa. There I had come to experience that, as Monroe proclaimed, I was indeed more than my physical body. And, as you now know, while at the Casa, I came to understand how true healing involved healing the split between body and spirit, the feminine and the masculine, that I'd encountered in Brazil. I found confirmation of my focus on feeling through my body to the energy that animates my physical form. With that said, I now offer a final ingredient of my daily spiritual practice and healing regimen. I use a variety of the Hemi-Sync CDs. My affirmation is as follows:

I AM more than my physical body and I AM now having a conscious beyond-my-finite physical body experience of [borrowing the phrase of Anita Moorjani in her book *Dying to be Me*] my infinite magnificent [and I add] multidimensional self."

Once Anita fully experienced her "infinite magnificent self," she was cured of her cancer. The twenty four lemon-sized tumors disappeared within days of her coming out of her coma. I wish you, dear reader, all the best on your healing journey to discover the vastness of just who you really are. . . .

www.ingramcontent.com/pod-product-compliance
Lightning Source LLC
Chambersburg PA
CBHW071144090426
42736CB00012B/2218